UNDERSTANDING AND FACILITATING THE ACHIEVEMENT OF AUTISTIC POTENTIAL

UNDERSTANDING AND FACILITATING THE ACHIEVEMENT OF AUTISTIC POTENTIAL

How to Effectively Support Children on the Autism Spectrum

DR EMMA GOODALL

Healthy Possibilities

Contents

This book is dedicated to all the people who have taught me;
my parents,
my wife,
my friends,
my son,
the students I have taught,
my whanau,
my mahi whanau,
my teachers from Elleray,
my boss at Johanna Primary School,
the disability advocates past, present and future
and the neurodiversity movement.

**Neurodiversity
is everywhere,
in infinite ways.**
Emma Goodall

2020

I

❧

Introduction

A version of this book was originally written in response to requests to provide some reference materials that contained practical strategies combined with easy to understand rationale. This updated version is specifically for Aotearoa and printed locally. I graduated as a teacher in the 1990's in the UK, and quickly discovered my love of teaching those quirky kids that other teachers often struggled with. I hungered for more understanding and more strategies for my students that I was unable to facilitate achievement for. After completing my Masters, focused on special education and equality of opportunity I designed and taught a special needs teaching paper for the Montessori Centre in London, England.

In the years since then, I have been diagnosed with Aspergers, worked for the Ministry of Education in Aotearoa/New Zealand, researched and written a PhD thesis around teachers and their students on the autistic spectrum and set up an Autism Spectrum consultancy. I recently worked in South Australia, initially with responsibility for all the children and students on the autism spectrum in state education, and then as the State Education system's Manager for Disability & Complex Needs. I now work for an Australia wide Not for Profit in the autism and diverse learners' space as their National Content & Resources Coordinator. A great job for one of the only openly autistic education autism advisors in the Southern Hemisphere. It does however mean being away from whanau and Aotearoa. ☹

My passion for meeting the needs of students of the autistic spectrum has been surpassed by my desire to help families, teachers and education systems to understand the potential of these students and how best to support autistic children and young people to achieve their potential.

I identify as autistic, with my specific diagnosis being Aspergers. Like most autistic adults, I choose to use the label autistic. This differs from the people first language of most disability advocates and relates to our acceptance and recognition of the pervasive nature of autism. I have blue eyes, I can change the colour of these with coloured contact lenses. I cannot change my autism, though I can learn strategies to maximise my potential and minimise my difficulties. For some autistics, more supports will be required and some autistics will have less independence in their daily living. Using this logic, we do not have autism as we cannot change it or hide it completely, we are autistic. For those of us who chose to use the word in this way it is not a negative statement, but a factual statement, explaining many of our characteristics and giving a clue about the effective supports we require to achieve our potential. Where the term autistic is used it is a descriptor to cover the whole autism spectrum. I hope that this book is both easy to understand and useful at a practical level. If you have any questions you can contact me via my blog/websites at:

https://healthypossibilities.net/ or https://mindfulbodyawareness.com/

It is important to note that although the number of students with a diagnosis on the autistic spectrum has increased dramatically, evidence suggests that the prevalence of autism spectrum in the adult population is similar to that found in children (Brugha, McManus, Bankart, Scott, Purdon, Smith, Bebbington, Jenkins, & Meltzer. 2011). The lack of a decrease in incidence with age is consistent with no increase in actual prevalence, but an increase in awareness and diagnosis. The understanding of the way females on the spectrum can present differently from males on the spectrum has led to an increase in numbers of both girls and women being diagnosed as autistic.

2

⁓❧⁓

Understanding the Autism Spectrum

Autism was first described by Kanner (1943) in his paper "Autistic Disturbances of Affective Contact" in the Journal *Nervous Child*. This study was based on eleven children who clearly demonstrated, among other things, a lack of joy in contact with their parents. This was quickly followed by Asperger's (1944) paper in German that involved the study of 200 families of similar children, though these children did not exhibit language delay. This paper was finally translated into English in 1989, although the term Asperger's Syndrome was already in use in the UK by then. The autism spectrum encompasses Asperger's, autism and PDD-NOS. It should be noted that there are two different diagnostic manuals in use in the western world, the DSM-V and the ICD-10. Asperger's is no longer recognised in the DSM-V but is in the ICD. The DSM-V additionally uses severity ratings for each of the two domains (Social Communication and Restricted and Repetitive Patterns of Behaviour Interests and Activities), ranging from Level 1 - Requiring Support to Level 3 – Requiring Very Substantial Support. However, these are less useful that might be initially thought, as autistic individuals may require very different levels of support depending on their immediate environment, demands being made and supports around them.

The knowledge and understanding of the autistic spectrum has varied over time and place, with for example the inaccurate suggestion in the 1960s that autism was caused by mothers being too cold and distant with their children. However, current research indicates that there are a range of autistic phenotypes within the spectrum with a strong genetic base. What this means is that researchers have proved that the autistic brain is different to a typical brain, and that children are born with these neurological differences, with a large range of genes implicated. What is key to the long-term outcomes for autistics is the way that they are supported to achieve their potential. If this is not done, sadly the effects on quality of life can be quite extreme, with rates of mental illness and suicidal ideation far higher for autistics than allistics (non-autistics).

Another important change in the way we understand and work with autistic children and adults has been the growth of lived experience information. This has led to some startling discoveries like the number of non-speaking autistics that when children were labelled as having an intellectual disability, who have gone on to teach themselves to read and type and even write books, attend university, run businesses, have friends and families and live good lives. Oral communication skills are not an indicator of innate intelligence, and may vary within a person over not just their lifetime but within each day.

The autistic spectrum encompasses people who are completely non-speaking to those who as adults regularly give public lectures or workshops or work as actors/actresses. It also encompasses people at all levels of intelligence as measured by IQ tests, or demonstrated through art, music, maths, science, IT etc. In other words, it encompasses the full range of people on our planet. What sets autistics apart from others is that the way their brains function is so different that it means the autistic experience and expression of that experience are different to that of others.

I will now explain the Autism Spectrum in three different ways; as a system of impairments or difficulties used for diagnosis (medical model), as a neurological difference (neurodiversity model) and what it means from a lived experience point of view.

The medical model of the autism spectrum

This model uses either the ICD10 or the DSM-V, which set out criteria that must be observed in a person for that person to be said to have autism. There are a range of screening and diagnostic tools in use around the world. In Aotearoa/New Zealand there are particular tools that should be used during the diagnostic process, in order to ensure that the same criteria are being applied to all children across the country. The American Psychiatric Association's Diagnostic and Statistical Manual-V (2013) contains the following information:

Diagnostic Criteria for 299.00 Autism Spectrum Disorder (requires criteria A-E)

1. Persistent deficits in social communication and social interaction across multiple contexts, as manifested by the following, currently or by history (examples are illustrative, not exhaustive; see text):

    1. Deficits in social-emotional reciprocity, ranging, for example, from abnormal social approach and failure of normal back-and-forth conversation; to reduced sharing of interests, emotions, or affect; to failure to initiate or respond to social interactions.

    2. Deficits in nonverbal communicative behaviours used for social interaction, ranging, for example, from poorly integrated verbal and nonverbal communication; to abnormalities in eye contact and body language or deficits in understanding and use of gestures; to a total lack of facial expressions and nonverbal communication.

    3. Deficits in developing, maintaining, and understand relationships, ranging, for example, from difficulties adjusting behaviour to suit various

social contexts; to difficulties in sharing imaginative play or in making friends; to absence of interest in peers.

Specify current severity: **Severity is based on social communication impairments and restricted, repetitive patterns of behaviour.**

1. Restricted, repetitive patterns of behaviour, interests, or activities, as manifested by at least two of the following, currently or by history (examples are illustrative, not exhaustive; see text):
    1. Stereotyped or repetitive motor movements, use of objects, or speech (e.g., simple motor stereotypes, lining up toys or flipping objects, echolalia, idiosyncratic phrases).
    2. Insistence on sameness, inflexible adherence to routines, or ritualized patterns of verbal or nonverbal behaviour (e.g., extreme distress at small changes, difficulties with transitions, rigid thinking patterns, greeting rituals, need to take same route or eat same food every day).
    3. Highly restricted, fixated interests that are abnormal in intensity or focus (e.g., strong attachment to or preoccupation with unusual objects, excessively circumscribed or perseverative interests).
    4. Hyper- or hypo reactivity to sensory input or unusual interest in sensory aspects of the environment (e.g. apparent indifference to pain/temperature, adverse response to specific sounds or textures, excessive smelling or touching of objects, visual fascination with lights or movement).

Specify current severity: **Severity is based on social communication impairments and restricted, repetitive patterns of behaviour.**

1. Symptoms must be present in the early developmental period (but may not become fully manifest until social demands exceed limited capacities, or may be masked by learned strategies in later life).
2. Symptoms cause clinically significant impairment in social, occupational, or other important areas of current functioning.
3. These disturbances are not better explained by intellectual disability (intellectual developmental disorder) or global developmental delay. Intellectual disability and autism spectrum disorder frequently co-occur; to make comorbid diagnoses of autism spectrum disorder and intellectual disability, social communication should be below that expected for general developmental level.

Note: Individuals with a well-established DSM-IV diagnosis of autistic disorder, Asperger's disorder, or pervasive developmental disorder not otherwise specified should be given the diagnosis of autism spectrum disorder. Individuals who have marked deficits in social communication, but whose symptoms do not otherwise meet criteria for autism spectrum disorder, should be evaluated for social (pragmatic) communication disorder.

Specify if:

- **With or without accompanying intellectual impairment**
- **With or without accompanying language impairment**
- **Associated with a known medical or genetic condition or environmental factor**
- **Associated with another neurodevelopmental, mental, or behavioural disorder**
- **With catatonia** (refer to the criteria for catatonia associated with another mental disorder)

Severity levels are illustrated in this table:

Level	Social communication difficulties	Restricted, repetitive patterns of behaviour.
Level 3 - "Requiring very substantial support"	Severe deficits in verbal and nonverbal social communication skills cause severe impairments in functioning, very limited initiation of social interactions, and minimal response to social overtures from others. For example, a person with few words of intelligible speech who rarely initiates interaction and, when he or she does, makes unusual approaches to meet needs only and responds to only very direct social approaches.	Inflexibility of behaviour, extreme difficulty coping with change, or other restricted/repetitive behaviours markedly interfere with functioning in all spheres. Great distress/difficulty changing focus or action.
Level 2 - "Requiring substantial support"	Marked deficits in verbal and nonverbal social communication skills; social impairments apparent even with supports in place; limited initiation of social interactions; and reduced or abnormal responses to social overtures from others. For example, a person who speaks simple sentences, whose interaction is limited to narrow special interests, and how has markedly odd nonverbal communication.	Inflexibility of behaviour, difficulty coping with change, or other restricted/repetitive behaviours appear frequently enough to be obvious to the casual observer and interfere with functioning in a variety of contexts. Distress and/or difficulty changing focus or action.
Level 1 - "Requiring support"	Without supports in place, deficits in social communication cause noticeable impairments. Difficulty initiating social interactions, and clear examples of atypical or unsuccessful response to social overtures of others. May appear to have decreased interest in social interactions. For example, a person who is able to speak in full sentences and engages in communication but who's to- and-fro conversation with others fails, and whose	Inflexibility of behaviour causes significant interference with functioning in one or more contexts. Difficulty switching between activities. Problems of organization and planning hamper independence.

attempts to make friends are odd and typically unsuccessful.	

Neurodiversity Model of the autism spectrum

The idea of Neurodiversity was developed by autistic people as a way of reframing the autism spectrum rather than accepting the medical model which pathologizes difference. Neurodiversity suggests that autistic people are not disordered at all rather they are differently ordered. Research has demonstrated that autistic brains are differently wired to non-autistic brains, this results in people who think differently.

The core idea within the neurodiversity model is that the autism spectrum is a neurological difference and that the key to living well on the autism spectrum is to be accepted for who you are and supported to develop the skills that will help you achieve your potential. According to the neurodiversity model the autism spectrum is not a condition to be cured. Rather it a way of being that is both useful and valid. Autistics seek to be understood and supported to achieve their autistic potential.

The US National Institutes of Health (http://www.ninds.nih.gov) suggest that "using advanced brain imaging techniques, scientists have revealed structural and functional differences in specific regions of the brains of children who have Asperger syndrome versus those who do not have the disorder. These differences may be caused by the abnormal migration of embryonic cells during foetal development that affects brain structure and "wiring" in early childhood and then goes on to affect the neural circuits that control thought and behaviour."

The autism spectrum has a range of neurological differences from typical brains and the resulting different development of the brain, causes difficulty with behaviour, communication, learning, and social interaction. There is a lot of research (Google brain scans or brain difference and autism for examples) about the neurological differences between neurotypical people and those on the autism spectrum. Although vaguely useful in that it confirms a life-long state of being, this does not advance understanding of what it means or feels like to experience life on the autistic spectrum. It does however, suggest that because autism has core neurological differences to non-autistic brains that autistics should be accepted for who they are and not forced to change. For example, just as a blind person would not be told to try harder to see, an autistic should not be told to make eye contact, stop being literal etc.

This model accepts that there are a range of difficulties associated with the autism spectrum but suggests that the person should not be asked to do things that will cause further distress, for example make eye contact with their teacher. Some researchers (Jaarsma & Welin, 2012) have suggested that this model is only valid for people who have fewer difficulties or struggles because of their autism. As an autistic, I would suggest that the idea of acceptance of autism as a valid way of experiencing and responding to the world is as useful for autistics at both ends of the spectrum.

Lived experience of the autism spectrum

Surprisingly lived experience of autism has not historically been accepted as a valid way of being an expert or even knowledgeable about autism. Adults on the autism spectrum who have put forward different explanations for children on the autism spectrum's behaviours have historically not been listened to. This has created a situation where allistic (non-autistic) professionals describe autism and how to support autistic children in fundamentally flawed ways. An example of this is the idea of routine. Many autistic people do indeed love routines, however many are able to cope with self-created change but not externally created change. Both are a break in routine, however in one control over self is maintained events are predictable but in the other control has been removed and there is a loss of predictability. Lived experience suggests that predictability and/or control over self and environment is the core issue rather than routine. Non-lived experience experts are still stuck on the idea of routine. Interestingly, parents are now advised not to have very proscribed routines so that their autistic children get used to change from early childhood. Although I agree with this, it does miss the point that control and/or predictability, rather than routine, is the important aspect for autistics.

Lived experience of autism suggests a variety of joys and struggles, much as for any person. Sadly however, there is a much higher incidence of bullying, loneliness and resultant distress. This distress can and does result in high levels of anxiety disorders, depression and suicide. Eliminating this distress by ensuring autistics are valued and cared for and about is one of the key factors in facilitating the achievement of autistic potential.

Non or partially-speaking autistics write about their frustration with being viewed as unintelligent, with the lack of understanding of their communication strategies. For example, many autistics flap their hands to communicate particular states of being/emotions. Lived experience of stimming (repetitive movements/actions) is one of using particular actions to self-calm or express distress. Others mis-understanding this and viewing stims as unacceptable has and continues to cause much distress to autistics.

The joy of hyper-focus on a special interest is possibly one of the nicest aspects of lived experience of autism, though it is close to the joy of positive sensory experiences. However, sensory or emotional overload are the opposite and some of the greatest struggles of being autistic.

For me growing up as an undiagnosed autistic, I was diagnosed in 2012; life was about being outside of the norm, a bit different from others. I was the proverbial nerd or geek, a bright girl who sat and the back and got really good exam results. Except, if I don't understand a concept right away, I often never get it. I have exceptional focus for things I am interested in and appalling focus for things I am not. I have had to learn social rules and etiquette. I believe in and use politeness, but it is a rule and I get offended when others are not polite. I can't read other people's intentions. I was in trouble a lot at school because I would not do what I was told unless I could see the point of doing so. I was hyperlexic (as are many autistic girls) and taught myself to read by age 3. I preferred adults or older/younger children to my peers. I usually only had one or two friends.

As a teenager, I was quite clearly odd, different to my peers. I had zero dress sense, no understanding of fashion, hated make-up and misunderstood and mis-applied large numbers of social rules. I love learning but hated the intensely social world of university. I prefer one to one interactions, or giving a lecture or presentation, but I hate the morning tea socialising. I have sensory sensitivities that limit what I eat, wear, touch, and these constantly affect my comfort and emotions. For example, wool itches me, so I won't touch it, let alone wear it. For me the tv is usually on so quietly that my partner can't hear it, but when it gets turned up to 'normal' volume, it sounds way too loud for me. Lights of the wrong type feel like they burn my eyeballs.

I am about to get married to my long-term partner, work full time in a senior role, have a PhD, raised a step child, have pets, hobbies. To outsiders I look and sound 'normal', but autism affects what I do, when I do it and how I do it. I have very poor facial recognition, learning who people are by their hairstyles. Every time a colleague gets her hairstyle changed; I have to relearn who she is. When overloaded I need to take time to calm or my mental and physical health can be affected. If I choose well, I can live a great life, full of healthy possibilities, however children do not have control over their environments and so may not have the opportunity to self-calm, and therefore are unable to achieve because of their overload.

To an outsider, I often seem very high functioning and in common with many other autistics can categorically say level of functioning is NOT fixed. When I am stressed or overloaded, in common with many others on the spectrum my functioning diminishes significantly. Additionally, my skill set is and always has been very varied. I am multi-lingual, a professional consultant and public speaker, but until very recently could not use a bus unless I had a map with me. If I was being observed when using public transport in an unfamiliar place I would be seen as quite low functioning, whereas if I was observed giving a workshop I would be labelled as high functioning.

<h1>3</h1>

<h1>Understanding the Autistic Experience</h1>

The way that people on the autistic spectrum experience their environment is different to the way that people who are not on the spectrum experience the world. It is important to note that experience is a combination of actual input from the outside of the human body, the brain's interpretation of this input combined with sensory input from inside the body (interoception) and the resultant perception of these. Interoception is atypical in autistics as well as those who have experienced trauma.

As an example, when you hear a noise, this noise is as a result of vibrations. The vibrations travel through the atmosphere. When these sound waves arrive at your ear, the shape of your ear directs the vibrations towards the inner ear and ear drum. The sound waves are detected as fluctuations in air pressure and are translated by the neural pathways into electrical signals for the brain to interpret. Your brain then interprets the directionality of the sound as well as the actual sound. Thus, when the school bell rings behind you, you know the sound is both behind you and that it is the school bell.

In addition, your brain uses prior experience and context to evaluate, prioritise and interpret sensory input. The autistic experience differs in both the brain's interpretation and the resultant perception. In the example of the bell, an autistic child may perceive the bell to be extremely loud or barely perceptible, whereas your perception is that it is quite loud but not overly so. Your brain will in addition have filtered out a number of competing background noises and prioritised the bell as being an important signal to the start of the school day. An autistic person struggles to filter sensory experiences and may be prioritising the leaf colours, light patterns on the floor or the sound of an ambulance from six blocks away.

The following picture of part of a leaf illustrates some of the different foci that autism can bring. The first picture is taken directly from a photo of a number of hostas, but the focus is on one particular leaf. The second one shows how light can be brighter for some autistics, the third how colours can be brighter, the fourth and forth photos show ever increasing foci on the detail of the leaf veins.

Light effecting details on hosta leaves
Emma Goodall 2013

Allistics usually have excellent sensory filters, whereas autistics have excellent sensors. We autistics often hear, see, feel everything, we notice all the small details. As illustrated above, the details on the hosta leaf were noticed with more intensity than the overall picture of the hostas and their setting in the garden. Autistics usually struggle to filter all the incoming sensory information and can develop strategies to cope that result in aspects of the details being prioritised because those aspects appeal on a personal level. With a poor ability to filter these inputs autistics can easily become overloaded. Instead of seeing the plants on the left, the autistic experience will be taking in more of the details with a resultant input like the image on the right.

Big picture versus detail visual input
Emma Goodall 2013

Imagine that you are in a large arena with 45,000 people all screaming and shouting, suddenly it starts to pour with rain, the stage lights start flashing, the rock band is playing a crowd favourite and then your cell phone dings quietly – announcing the arrival of an important text message. How likely are you to notice the message?

For autistic children the classroom can feel like the scenario above and the teacher's instructions sound as quiet as a cell phone ding during a rock concert. Open plan schools or modular classrooms can be particularly difficult for autistic students as they can't filter all the incoming noises to consistently prioritise their teacher's voice over all the other incoming noises. Ensuring the environment is quiet before trying to engage with the autistic student will directly increase the likelihood of effective engagement.

Even with a quiet room in terms of sound, the environment can be busy, which can create visual or tactile noise for the autistic student. Some autistic students are sensitive to air pressure, which means seating needs to take into account fluctuations in air pressure for seats by doorways or in the direct line of air flow from a heat pump. Other autistic students will seek out warmth or coolness, and so would benefit from these seats!

Additionally, most autistics are sensitive to the other people in the environment, their movements and actions as well as their voices. What is less well known is that most autistics are also extremely sensitive to the emotions around them. Although it is difficult for autistics to recognise, interpret and label the body language of others as emotions, they can sense these emotions very strongly. As a result, an autistic student may sense the underlying sadness or anger of a teacher, despite that teacher smiling and pretending to be happy. Emotionally sensitive autistic students can appear to 'take on' the emotions of others, for example crying when a peer is crying, or they can become inconsolable when there is a lot of conflict or anger in the air.

The combination of others, their emotions, the environment and the noise within it can lead the autistic student to overload easily and frequently. To diminish those 'aggggh' moments for autistic students reducing the noise and busyness of the environment are the easiest strategies. It is difficult to change people's emotions or the smells and sights of others within the school. The provocation of aggggggggggggh for autistic students is caused by:

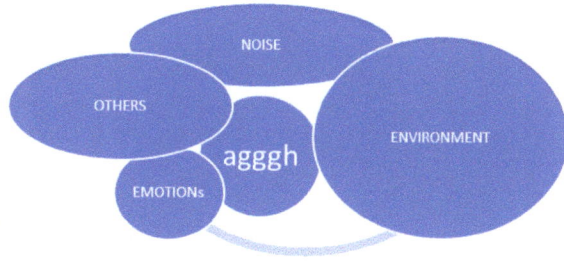

Contextual factors of overload
Emma Goodall 2015

In addition, atypical interoception results in muted or hyper-awareness of internal body signals and muted or hyper-accuracy of these signals. So, for some autistics they are not really aware of their muscles and cannot feel the difference between a stretched and a relaxed muscle. Additional issues can be related to muted/hyper awareness of pain, difficulty in pinpointing where pain is even if the pain is noticed, not being aware of bladder/bowel fullness, atypical awareness and responses to thirst and hunger. Atypical interoception means that often autistics struggle to be aware of feelings and emotions until they become 'big emotions/feelings'. This results in it looking like an autistic goes from being fine to exploding in a split second. In reality, they just did not know that their emotion was building up and they sympathetic nervous system response was becoming more intense. Once they enter sympathetic nervous system overload they go into flight/fight/freeze/flop or drop – externalizing or internalising their overload.

4

Understanding the Autistic Brain

One of the main characteristics of the autistic brain is also the key to effective engagement of autistic students. The cartoon below illustrates this characteristic, which results in autistics wanting to know everything about a topic or not being interested at all in a topic or task. This characteristic links with the detail focus of autistics, so that when studying a topic of utter obsession an autistic student will be motivated to learn not just major facts about something, but all related trivia.

Like a light switch; interest and engagement is either on or off.
Emma Goodall 2013

Another major characteristic of the autistic brain is the way it processes social information differently. A group of very young students are often able to sense the relative social importance of different people, whereas autistic students may never be able to understand or respond to the concept of relative social status. Generally, young people perceive a social status hierarchy where the higher the status, the more important it is to listen to and follow instructions from a person. In this case, for example, what a peer says is less important than what the teacher says, which is less important than what the principal says. This results in situations where students know they should not do something because the teacher told them not to, even when a peer has told them to do it.

However, autistic students (and adults) do not recognise social status hierarchies as valid categories. Instead, all living beings are viewed as equal, with the possible exception of self as more important than others, which is a natural developmental stage of all human beings. Many autistic students (and adults) perceive that animals have the same value as humans and that all humans are equal in worth. This creates difficulties in situations where an autistic student is given conflicting instructions by different people. The instructions are perceived to be coming from equal sources, and so it is hard for the student to make the socially correct choice.

At the same time, a massive sense of social justice is present in most autistics students (and adults). Because all people (or all living beings) are perceived as equal, injustice is abhorrent and highly distressing to autistics. This can present as an autistic student being the class police officer, always trying to enforce rules and tell other students off. Whilst being in this role, the autistic student is often doing things the teacher says they shouldn't; such as shouting.

Trying to ensure everyone follows the rules
Emma Goodall 2013

The autistic student is trying to enforce rules and social justice because they do not realise that the teacher is responsible for this. In their mind, everyone is responsible for this. As they grow older this idea that everyone is responsible for social justice and harmony becomes more prevalent in society, so it is important not to negate this understanding in younger autistic children. An effective method for managing this policing behaviour in young autistic students is to give them a clip board, on which they can draw or write everything that they perceive is wrong or unjust during the day. At pre-arranged times during the day, such as just before lunch and at the end of the day, the student is allocated time to present their clipboard to the teacher. In this way the teacher does not constantly have to respond to the student and they are able to work towards achieving social justice. It is important to note that this will only work if the teacher follows up any serious breaches of school rules or unkind behaviours. See the section on supporting positive behaviour for more information.

Another key thinking style that impact teaching and learning is the autistic feeling that 'now is forever'. This means that when you ask an autistic to stop reading and come and do maths, they think that you mean they will never be able to read again and will be doing maths forever. I often illustrate this point with a story about my move to Australia. We moved over to Australia on Christmas eve in 2013. By Jan 2nd, 2014, I was convinced that because I had not yet managed to get a job in Australia, that I would never get a job there and that my PhD focused on teaching students on the autism spectrum was useless. Within another two weeks I had got a job, but for those two weeks nothing could convince me that this was possible!

People on the autism spectrum perceive, understand and interact with the world differently than neurotypical people. Don't forget how they interact with the world is normal for them. As discussed this is because they hear, see, taste, smell, touch and feel differently to NTs. Research from Baron-Cohen, Ashwin, Ashwin, Tavassoli & Chakrabarti, (2009) has validated the idea that autistic people's senses (including sensing emotion) are more acute that that of other people. This acuity of sense in conjunction with difficulty filtering input and atypical interoception is what often leads to behaviours that others perceive as challenging, but is sympathetic nervous system overload.

On a positive note, between 5-10% of children on the autism spectrum have been estimated to be hyperlexic (i.e. teach themselves to read before they start school), with autistic girls are more likely to be hyperlexic than any other children. Some of these hyperlexic children DO understand both fiction and non-fiction texts and some only understand non-fiction. However, finding out what they understand is not always straightforward. This is because the autistic child is often close to overload and so will try not to engage in any processing that is not either highly interesting to them or necessary. Many autistic students (and adults) also have auditory and/or language processing disorders, which can make it difficult for them to understand and respond to questions in a timely manner. Students with limited spoken language skills may well be able to read in their heads but not say the words out loud.

- The autistic brain is hyper logical and language is initially understood literally with idioms being learnt one by one. Written words are often learnt as sight words rather than phonetically. Children may understand words but be unable to explain them to others verbally.
- Autistic children interpret questions in a two-step process; am I psychologically able to respond to this question and if so, what does the question logically mean? This can be problematic when it comes to ascertaining understanding because the autistic student may not have enough energy left to answer. If they do go on to process the question about what happened in a story you have both just read, logically the question is pointless, as you should know already, because you read it too, therefore there is no need to answer!

It is generally accepted that children learn best when they are emotionally and physically safe and have all their needs met. For autistic children this is very difficult to achieve as the busy school environment can interfere with their readiness to learn. Additionally, because many autistics are visual learners but the medium of most education is spoken there is a mismatch between learning and teaching styles.

5

What is Autistic Potential?

I am endlessly fascinated by the lack of mainstream awareness of the potential of autistics. I work with families who think their autistic child will not be able to go to university, hold down a job or enjoy a relationship. I meet autistic children who are not seen to have the potential to read or type because they are currently non-speaking.

I am not an anomaly. I am not atypical for an autistic, I work, have a PhD, am married to my long-term partner, helped raise a child, run a business etc. Most of the autistics that I know in person or online have degrees, have had or are in long term relationships, have had or do have successful careers. I know autistics studying part time at university and/or doing volunteer work, I know non-speaking autistic adults who write prose far better than I could ever hope to. Why, I wonder, are these autistic potentials not understood and shared in the wider world outside of our autistic community?

More than this, I question why some of us experience more anxiety or less confidence than others. Minimising anxiety and maximising confidence seem to be key components of achieving autistic potential. I was brought up to believe I could have any career I wanted, I was expected to go to university. When other people put me down or said I could not achieve something, I presumed they were stupid, because I believed in my own competence. I believed in myself because my parents and teachers believed in me. Yes, I admit, I am one of those academic nerdy people, loved learning at school etc etc. But before you think, well my student or child could not achieve anything, pause a moment and reflect:

- Autistic adults who are non-speaking can read and type, writing powerful and emotive poetry, stories and non-fiction (Amy Sequenzia, Carly Fleischmann)
- Autistics who were non-speaking until they started school have gone on to lecture at university, write books, make lots of money (Temple Grandin)
- Autistic adults who lacked interest in many aspects of school and focused on their strengths and interests go on to develop incredible skills in their areas of

interest, many of which enable these adults to pursue careers in these areas (the Pokemon inventor Satoshi Tajiri)

- Stroppy autistic girls can grow into strong secure autistic women, gaming fanatic Autistic boys can grow into computer programmers who make more money in a week than many people many in a year

Our autistic potential exists because we naturally want to spend time doing things, we are interested in. This is often described as obsessing or fixating, but if that interest turns into a career is that obsession healthy or unhealthy? Our autistic potential also exists because of our natural attention to detail and desire to perfect the things that we choose to do. Perfectionism can be a curse, but the drive behind it can propel us into success.

Our autistic potential is hindered when we lack self-belief or others lack belief in us. But even more crucially our potential can be blocked by anxiety and sensory overload. It is not possible to learn and grow if you are constantly stressed and anxious or spending all your energy trying to deal with sensory overload.

I wore headphones all through university, at school my classrooms were quiet, and I could learn. Some classrooms I visit now are so vibrant, busy and full of children collaboratively discussing their work that I need to leave within an hour. I have a choice, an autistic student may not... How are they supposed to learn, to develop their autistic potential when they are overloaded by the vibrancy and busyness of their classroom? As a result, these autistic children do not appear to make progress and/or exhibit challenging behaviours. Often, these very same children will read incessantly at home, but struggle to read basic books at school.

Autistic kids have another barrier to achieving their potential. They, I included, often refuse(d) to do school tasks they perceive as pointless/boring/way too easy. Their teachers often think the students are not working because they don't know what to do or how to do it, when in fact they are too bored to do it (Attwood, 2011)!

Many Autistic kids and adults have an innate arrogance about their intelligence (Attwood, 2011) which they may or may not share with others (both of which have drawbacks). Because of this arrogance they often do not feel it is worthwhile doing things that are not interesting or challenging. These are the children making and selling computer games or jewellery or studying archaeology age 8-10, but doing very little at school. One of the reasons I loved school so much was that I was given work at my own level, so maths and Latin 3-5 years above my age, but English the same as my peers. I was also allowed to do a special interest project every term in my primary years. In high school I would spend hours and hours at home on my art projects and five minutes on all the rest of my homework combined. Introducing new skills and topics via special interests gets around this issue and pitching work too hard not too easy is more likely to engage an autistic child. Setting practical rather than written assignments may work for autistics who struggle to write.

But mostly, the most important facilitator for the achievement of autistic potential is having a belief in the competence and potential of autistic students (Goodall, 2013). Sharing stories of autistic adults and the range of abilities and careers they have will normalise the idea of working in a variety of capacities. Teaching strategies to succeed facilitates success. No-one needs to talk to be intelligent, it is others who need to learn to listen to unspoken words. No-one needs good facial recognition to be able to learn calculus. What autistic students need is to be interested and engaged. Good teachers and kind parents can drive the achievement of autistic potential by using topics that interest their autistic students and presentation methods that engage these students. Universities and employers can continue to facilitate autistics achieving their potential by being clear about their expectations, saying what they mean, meaning what they say and having low sensory environments. This minimises our anxiety and sensory inputs so that we can work hard, using our innate drive to learn, do, master things and achieve.

Autistic children also need to be resilient in order to reach their potential. Without resilience, it is hard for children to thrive and overcome difficulties or failures. The is the case both at home and at school.

> *Resilience is essentially the capacity to 'bounce back' fairly quickly after a difficulty or adverse experience. Resilience basically involves working through any challenges or difficulties encountered in a proactive manner that will enable you to build confidence and mastery in overcoming that difficulty. Through doing this, a person can build mastery and confidence in other areas of their life, without even realising that they are doing so.*
>
> *People who never have to face adversity or overcome challenges do not have the opportunities to develop resilience and are more likely to struggle long term with even minor difficulties than people who have developed resilience as they have grown up. This means that parents, families and educators all have roles to play in helping children experience, manage and overcome difficulties in ways that naturally scaffold the development of resilience. (Purkis & Goodall, 2017)*

Examples of autistic potential

Amy Sequenzia

Amy Sequenzia: When I had to struggle to be seen as a sentient being, as a thinking person, my self-esteem could not find room to manifest itself. I was constantly looking down at myself because that's how I was looked at. There were no expectations for me to fulfil because I was "nothing".

Today, despite many obstacles and doubters, I have a tribe of friends who value me, who help me when I need, who have my back. I am reminded that many want to hear from me and that my words and my life matter. My self-esteem can grow now and this makes me "look good".

When my friends, the ones I only see once a year, see me and think there was a big exterior transformation, they are actually seeing a confident me. It is not a miracle and it is not magic. I simply know that I can always believe in myself, that other people do believe in me, even on my bad seizure days, when it seems I will never be able to do anything ever again.

The presumption of my competence has spread from a few people to many more. When the world is so unprepared for how we do things, we do need friends and allies to help us navigate the obstacles. That's when presuming competence becomes practical. Instead of moving alone, living in silence, we want to keep reaching out because we know we are seen as equal by a growing number of people. Instead of being pitied, we experience understanding and high expectations. We do our best to fulfil these expectations and we feel energized by the feeling of accomplishment and the support from friends. We don't want to hide anymore. And we feel better. It shows externally. I think I do look good, better every year. Presumption of competence is better than any makeover! https://ollibean.com/2013/07/11/presumption-competence/

Carly Fleischmann

My name is **Carly Fleischmann** and as long as I can remember I've been diagnosed with autism. I am not able to talk out of my mouth; however, I have found another way to communicate by spelling on my computer. **(and yes, that is me typing on the computer by myself).** I used to think I was the only kid with autism who communicates by spelling but last year I met a group of kids that communicate the same way. In fact, some are even faster at typing then I am. http://carlysvoice.com/home/aboutcarly/

In the autumn of 2013, Carly started a Bachelor of Arts program from the University of Toronto. Carly and her family report that she has long surpassed the expectations of medical opinion, when Carly was a small child, which was that she would never develop intellectually beyond the mental age of a small child.

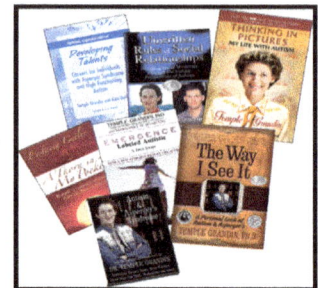

Temple Grandin – renown author and university professor, non-verbal until age four

A selection of Temple Grandin's books

6

◈

Before starting school

Many autistic children will go to pre-school, some will begin to receive extra support at this early age. Some children on the autism spectrum tend to receive their diagnosis and support earlier than others because of the difference in oral skills or behaviour. This section will be useful for children, whether or not they attended pre-school. This is because school is very different from pre-school and requires a whole new set of experiences, interactions and expectations.

Getting to know the school environment

Once a child has been enrolled at a school, it is important for them to be able to view the school when it is quiet before visiting during a normal school day. Parents can walk around the grounds with their child after school or at the weekend. Photos should be taken of key parts of the school and a pictorial map can be created at home with the photos. Older children could make their own maps. If a child will be attending an online school, they will need to be given time to get to know the way the online classroom works – how it looks and how to navigate it, prior to 'meeting' the teacher and being required to take part in lessons.

Meeting the teacher

A child's first meeting with their first teacher is an important event in any child's life, whether this is online or in person. For autistic children it is very important that this first meeting is positive, and the child feels welcome. People on the autistic spectrum are said not to respond to social cues, however most of them are extremely good at sensing other's emotions and attitudes. If a child on the spectrum feels that their teacher does not like them, this usually leads to a complete breakdown in relationship, followed by work and/or school refusal and/or raised anxiety, distress and can lead to depression, even in young children. This can be very problematic for teachers as it means if they themselves are angry or upset and mask this with a smile, most of the class will see the smile and be reassured that their teacher is happy (with them). However, the autistic child will often not notice the smile and instead senses the anger or upset, which they often then assume is directed at them.

In contrast, it is extremely easy to make an autistic child feel welcome. Greet them with genuine warmth, saying hello and using their name and then asking them their special interest (which you have confirmed with their family beforehand). Some examples;

"Hi Robbie. Nice to meet you. I am looking forward to being your teacher. Can you tell me a bit about what you like to make with Lego?"

"Hello Susie (signs hello). Welcome to our classroom (whilst signing welcome). Would you like me to read you Cinderella (holding out Susie's favourite book Cinderella)?"

When the child and their family leave, it will help to form a strong relationship if the teacher reiterates how much she/he is looking forward to being the child's teacher. The date and length of the next visit should also be stated explicitly. A photo of the teacher, classroom door (from outside) and classroom should be sent home with the child, so they can familiarise themselves with these key aspects of school.

For online education, it is helpful for the teacher to send a welcome video message or email to the student. In this, the teacher should mention something that they know the student is interested in. For example, if Josh in interested in engines, the teacher could say something about how they interact with engines in their life, or how much they are looking forward to learning about engines through working with Josh.

Meeting the class

Fostering a sense of belonging is important to the achievement of autistic potential, so how the child meets their new classmates should be planned. Ideally the class should view the child as competent and the child should view the class in a positive light. The type of communication the autistic student uses and their particular sensory sensitivities will influence how this first meeting proceeds. If the class is all online or distance education, 'meeting' their peers is still an important part of feeling a sense of belonging. In these cases, there can be video or text based messaged from the class to the new student or a collection made of interesting and relevant facts about the class, which is sent to the new student.

Additional considerations are;

- Do the family want their child's diagnosis and difference to be talked about with the class or not?
- Is the child more comfortable watching before joining in?

- If the child signs or uses a picture communication system, has the class learnt to some of this first? Or if the class is online, how is communication going to be facilitated and take place?
- Does the child need to sit with their body against a firm surface? (due to poor core muscles or other sensory difficulties). If the child is being educated online form home, how physically tiring is it for them to access the computer for long periods of time? If this is not manageable, what period of time is optimal, how else can the child be engaged in the learning?
- Are there sounds/visual inputs that are highly distressing to the child?
- Does the child have prosopagnosia (inability to recognise faces) or some degree of difficulty with this (estimates are that up to half the people on the autistic spectrum have difficulty recognising faces)?

Because children often notice difference, they can respond to this difference with incredible kindness and support or with unkindness that can lead to bullying. It is vital to foster a sense of class belonging and to ensure students all feel responsible for one another so that playground and/ or online bullying is prevented by the class, rather than ignored or supported.

Introduction to school routines and daily timetable

Visual supports are ideal for introducing school routines and the daily timetable to autistic spectrum children. Older children, or those who are able to read may prefer their supports to be written words, rather than pictures. The use of both through labelled pictures can ensure the same visual supports can be used for a range of children over a number of years. This facilitates continuity of meaning for the students and makes it easier for schools and individual teachers to set up these systems.

The degree to which a student requires support to learn school routines and gain an understanding of the daily timetable varies considerably. School and family need to work together to assume competence and teach towards that. The level of independence being aimed for should be the highest realistically possible, whilst trying to avoid anxiety and distress. For example, if the child is physically able to hang their bag up, this should be the goal, whereas if this is not possible either this needs to be done with another person or a solution found that can be achieved independently.

Laminated A4/A5 routine cards can be made up for each of the routines. These can be enlarged and displayed in the classroom/cloakroom/toilets/lunch area. The smaller size cards can be given to the students as prompts to follow for each of the routines. It is important to note that a child who follows the class, copying what they do, may not have learnt or understood the actual routine, but that they have developed a great strategy to work around that.

Examples of routines:

- Arriving at school in the morning – put your reading folder in the reading folder box, put your water bottle in the water bottle box, hang your bag up on your peg, go outside to play until the bell goes, when the bell goes, put your hat on your peg, come and sit on the mat looking at your teacher.
- Morning tea time – when the bell goes listen to your teacher, when the teacher says you can go, go to the toilet, wash your hands, get your lunch box, go and sit outside the classroom, eat your morning tea, when the bell goes put your lunch box back in your bag, go and play outside, when the bell goes again, go and line up outside your classroom, when the teacher says go inside, so and sit on the mat looking at your teacher.
- Hand washing (usually displayed above the sink/basin in the toilet area) – Turn on the tap, put your hands under the water, put soap on your hands, rub together, put hands under the tap again, when soap is washed off your hands turn tap off, dry your hands.

Each of these instructions will require a visual prompt (photo or other type of picture or symbol) with a written label. If the autistic child uses sign you may have photos of the signs as well as, or instead of the pictures. Introducing the daily timetable is most effective with whole class visuals. These are arranged in a highly visible and uncluttered part of the classroom, such as at the side of the white board, and referred to throughout the day.

Students can be provided with their own copies if they find it difficult to understand what is happening next or later on in the day. Examples of visuals are shown. These can be photocopied and laminated to be used in your classroom. When using a visual daily timetable, it is important to ensure that it is displayed either left to right or top to bottom, where left or top is the first part of the day and right or bottom depicts the end of the day. This directionality is important because large numbers of autistic students have sequencing difficulties. Following on from the visuals are a number of different examples of a daily visual timetable using these visuals as well as visual planner examples for fluent readers.

Numeracy

Group reading

Silent reading

Writing

Science

ICT

PE

Biology

Example visuals for visual timetable (photocopiable)

Emma Goodall 2020

History

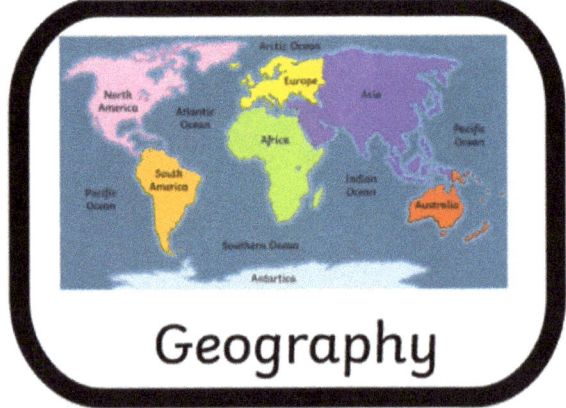

Geography

Art

Recess

Music

Assembly

Lunch

Construction

Further example visuals for visual timetable (photocopiable)

Emma Goodall 2020

Intermediate and High School routines

It can be very difficult for students to manage at intermediate and high school, with the introduction of different teachers in different classrooms for different subjects. Students may need to carry large amounts of books and 'stuff' to school and around school with them every day, if they are physically attending school. There are numerous opportunities to lose things and get lost. When transition is being planned, it is important to incorporate the daily routines from the new setting into any transition book or video. If the young person is learning online or via distance education, the timetable can be more complex and the changeovers between subjects very difficult. Topic based learning can be used to mitigate this, especially if the topic is an area of interest or passion for the young person.

It is a reasonable accommodation to allow a student to start early or late and leave early or late, whether that is each class or the whole day. This accommodation enables students to move about without being in a very large group that they may find overwhelming. Not all autistic students will need or want this, and some manage fine at transitions. Uniform rules often have hidden curriculum modifications and it can help autistic students to fit in, if they know what these are. For example, many students may wear black trainers rather than shoes or hair in styles that 'push the rules'. Online rules about group chats or group work may be impossible for autistic teens to manage without significant scaffolding. It would be a reasonable accommodation to minimize or not use group work, instead focusing on either individual or occasional paired work.

7

Visual supports

This section is applicable in the home as well as at school. Where students are being educated at home, the same types of visual supports can be used for 'school' as well as activities of daily living. Some students require support to know what tasks to do and to understand the routine of the school day. These are often students that are unable to stay on task for more than thirty seconds without support, or students who are highly distractible. The most basic type of planner for these students is a first then planner. When this is used the first activity should be the less preferred activity and the second activity one that the student is known to enjoy. Autistic students can become fixated on time and they interpret instructions literally, so it may help to add "until an adult says stop" onto the first/then planner, whether visually or in writing. When using visuals it is important to ensure the child has the same understanding of the visual as you do. For some children and young people, photos will need to be used, whilst others will be fine with icons or other types of drawings, and those who can read my prefer visuals with words only.

FIRST | THEN

handwriting

playground

UNTIL AN ADULT SAYS STOP

Example of a first/then visual
Emma Goodall 2013

FIRST	THEN	10Min
Numeracy	ICT	STOP

First/then and finally stop visual
Emma Goodall 2020

8

❦

Multi-step visuals

Once a student is able to work successfully with a first/then planner they can use multi-step visual planners and/or choice boards. Multi-step planners usually incorporate a finished box or envelope next to the planner so that when the student has finished each task on the planner it the visual for that task is placed in the finished box/envelope.

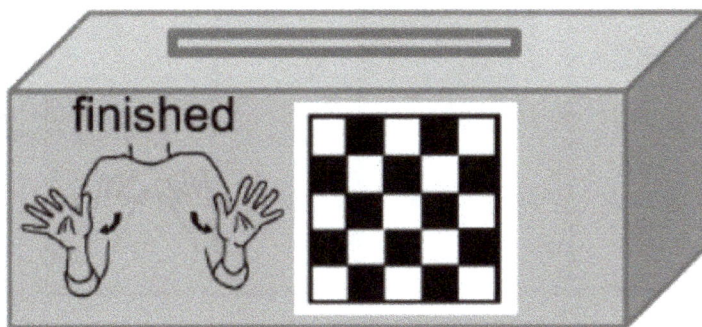

Finished box with visuals
Emma Goodall 2013

33

Morning routines visuals
http://www.setbc.org/pictureset/resources/arriving_at_school/
arriving_at_school.pdf

Morning routine example
Emma Goodall 2013

Washing hands

	Water on
	Hands wet
	Rub hands with soap
	Rinse
	Water off
	Dry

Washing hands visual prompt
http://www.setbc.org/pictureset/resources/hand_washing_routine/hand_washing_routine.pdf

Daily timetable visual planners

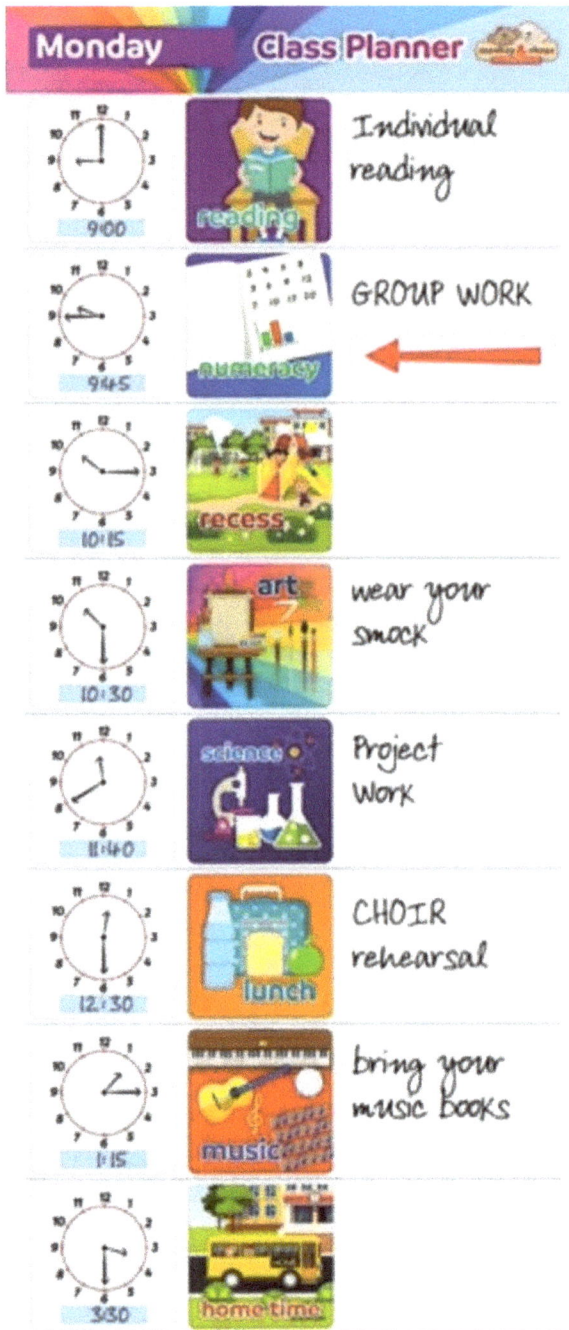

Daily timetable

Using freely available icons/symbols or pictures schools can design their own set of visuals to populate class and individual planners. It can be helpful to have a large set up that the whole class are directed to look at each day and a smaller set of identical pictures that are able to be used by individual students. In this case the individual set will be placed on a grid using bluetick or Velcro dots, so that they match the whole class set. This can be done with the individual child at the start of the day until they are able to do this by themselves.

The student is directed to place their visual timetable on their desk or next to them wherever they are working. If it is attached to a clipboard, the visual timetable can be taken outside when there are outdoor activities. The student can put each activity card into a finished box once the teacher indicates it is time to transition to the next activity. In this way, the student gains a sense of moving through the school day, but also a sense of accomplishment that they have participated in the same activities as their peers.

Some students, particularly those at high school or confident readers, will be happy with a colour coordinated timetable, and may not need any other visual supports. The timetable could be paper, electronic or programmed into their phone diary, or a combination of any of these.

* * *

Some schools are happy to colour code subjects and paint the room doors accordingly, with students able to have a book cover that matches the door that matches the timetable.

Younger or non-reading students may prefer a visual timetable like this one:

mat time	news	writing	morning tea
reading	maths	singing	Lunch

Visual timetable up to recess
Emma Goodall 2013

The afternoon timetable is presented only when lunch time is about to begin, so that the students are not overwhelmed with a long list of events/tasks. For some children, breaking the day into three and just presenting up to morning tea/recess, then up to lunch and then to the end of the day, will be appropriate.

| circle time | thinking skills | fitness | home time |

Visual timetable for the afternoon sessions
Emma Goodall 2013

Other types of visual supports can be things like visual timers that help develop the concept of how long different segments of time are. One way to understand the difficulty with the concept of the 'length' of time, is to think about the different experience of 5mins when you are in a traffic jam, versus when you are relaxed at home. In one instance five minutes can feel much longer than in the other instance. For some autistics, time usually has this flexible quality, whereby it can seem to be fleeting, stand still or last forever. Visual timers should not continue to be used if they create more anxiety, as for some autistics, this can happen.

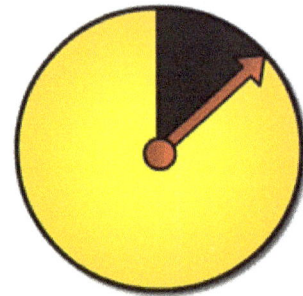

Use the Clock Timer Full Screen

Different types of visual timers

9

Transitioning from one activity to another

There are many reasons why transitions are difficult for autistic people, including perfectionism, which leads to a drive to finish one activity before starting another, a need to feel in control of their environment and a sense of now if forever. Being autistic results in a more intense experience of the world than for neurotypical people, this often results in difficulty processing the newest experience/event for the autistic person. To make transitions as easy and stress free as possible it is important that the student knows what is going to be happening and when it is going to be happening (predictability). Although a visual timetable does signal these things, many children on the autistic spectrum have difficulty sequencing and relating to time. This means that the visual timetable requires additional input just before and at transition times. Students will manage transitions better if they are signaled in advance with instructions (visual or oral) about what to do.

In some classrooms students return to the mat between activities, where the teacher introduces and often summarizes the task just finished and/or models the upcoming activity. If your classroom is managed like this, this is an ideal time to have a quick interoception break. Interoception activities help many children to refocus and self-regulate, not just children on the autistic spectrum. The most effective type of break will depend on the type of interoception the particular student benefits from most. See the section on Calming and self-calming.

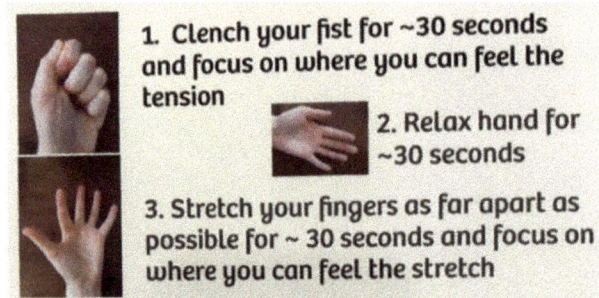

1. Clench your fist for ~30 seconds and focus on where you can feel the tension

2. Relax hand for ~30 seconds

3. Stretch your fingers as far apart as possible for ~ 30 seconds and focus on where you can feel the stretch

Calming card from Mindfulbodyawareness.com
Emma Goodall 2016

Ways to signal transitions

1. Clap hands or make a specific sound (i.e. a triangle or soft drum) 5 minutes before transition saying, "In 5 minutes we need to stop what we are doing". Repeat 1 minute before transition saying, "In 1 minute we need to stop what we are doing".

2. Tap student on shoulder or top of arm (if they are ok with being touched) 5 minutes before transition saying, "In 5 minutes we need to stop what we are doing". Repeat 1 minute before transition saying, "In 5 minutes we need to stop what we are doing".

3. Use a timer for the student, which sits where they can see it. Some students will reset timers if they want to work longer or want to stop working, so you may prefer a sand timer that is not within reach but can still be seen. Please not some students become fixated on timers to the exclusion of being able to work!

At transition time

Give explicit instructions on transitioning, these can be oral, pictorial or using a set visual prompt. Do not expect an autistic student to know when you want things putting away or handing in to you, or to process a generalised class instruction during a transition time. Examples of set visual prompts are given below. These can be handed to the student at transition time.

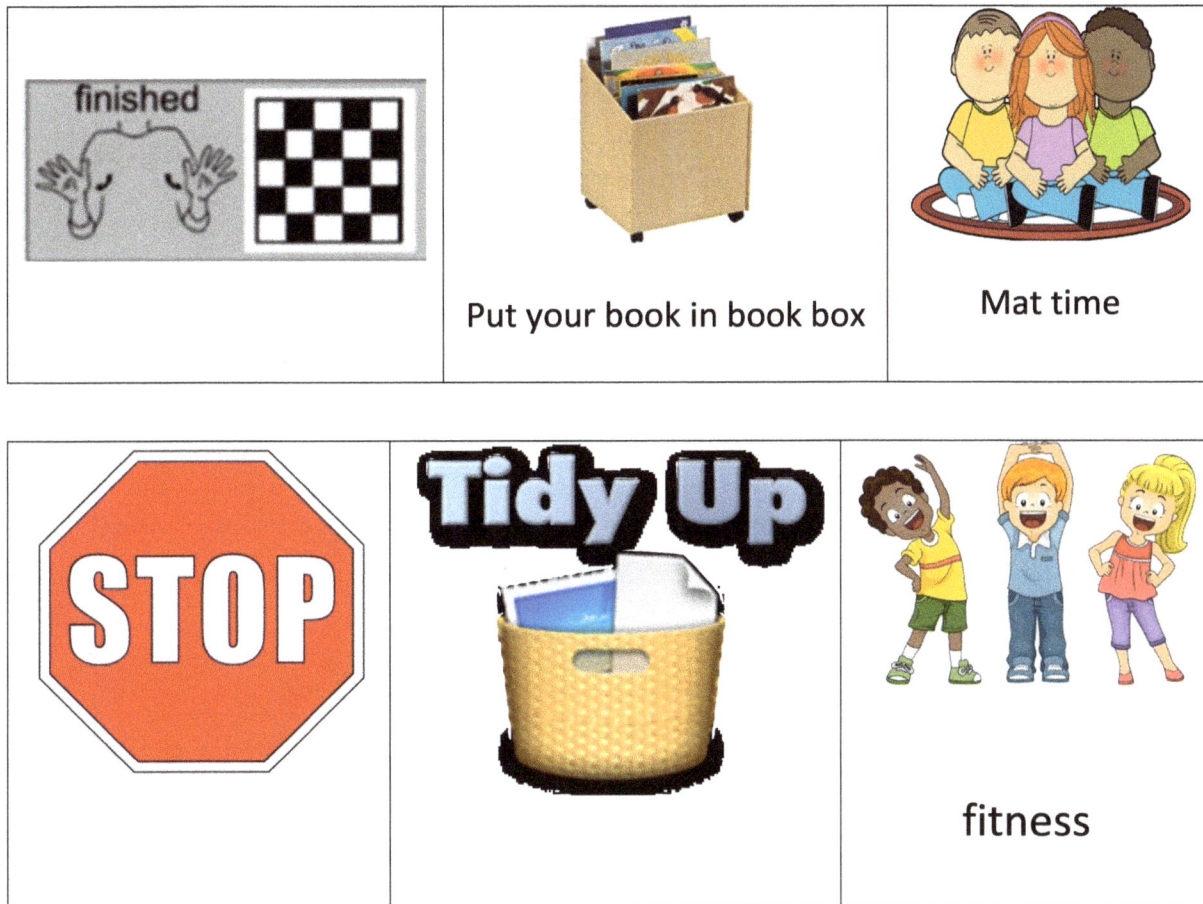

Example of visuals for signalling transitions
Emma Gooodall 2013

These visuals explain what to do in steps, stop the current activity, then tidy up/hand book in/ put books away etc and then were to transition to, e.g. mat time or fitness. These visuals will need to be supported by verbal and/or physical prompts initially, so that the student understands the visuals and what they are for. Once the student can follow the visuals with prompting, prompting should be slowly withdrawn in a manner that promotes independence.

This means that on days where the autistic student is stressed or overloaded, that they are given more prompting. On days where the student is calm, confident and/or content, the teacher provides less overt prompting. This could be simply tapping the visual to indicate the student needs to follow this visual now versus talking the student through each step and physically showing them where to go and what to do.

For some children and young people, change can be so jarring that it is helpful to signal in advance that a transition or change is coming. Change should always be signaled as a possibility with multi-activity/task timetables. For example, you may have a cut out no or stop sign that you can place over an activity that can no longer take place. Introducing this, or even a specific change sign or symbol should be done explicitly, so that children know "change happens, and that's ok, we will just do something different."

The stop or no symbol can be placed over the activity, task or object that will no longer be available, for example; no phone at the moment. This may be because the phone battery has died. An alternative may be offered such as a laptop. So the visual would look like:

A visual signaling change - no phone, computer instead
Emma Goodall 2020

10

Autistic communication strategies

It has been suggested (Winter, 2013) that the autistics may not always know that they need to communicate or indeed that it is possible to communicate. Once the idea of communicating has been taught at its most basic the autistic child will then know that communicating a need should result in that need being met. This level of understanding of communication is why it is important to always respond positively to initial communication attempts by children on the autism spectrum.

Some children will arrive at school using sign language, PECS (a picture exchange communication system), whilst others may use sign or oral language or an alternative AAC system such as Proloquo2go. Some autistic children will arrive with minimal oral language and no communication strategy beyond shouting or using flight/fight instincts. All these children will need support to maximise their communication skills and work towards their potential. Effective inclusion that welcomes all students will be most clearly visible through whole school communication strategies. If there are students that sign or use PECS then the whole school should also learn how to communicate via sign or PECS so that the student is able to engage with any/all students and staff.

Parents, teachers and family members can use really simple communication techniques like pointing, using photographs to offer choices of things that are not in the room. Some children like music and can express themselves through their choices of songs and other music, for example picking a particular song to play from mum's phone when happy and another when sad.

Signing

There are a number of different sign languages, each is a language in its own right. There are national sign languages, such as New Zealand, British and American Sign Languages. In addition, there is Makaton, which is a simplified signing system that was developed in Britain and has now been adapted and is used in over fifty countries.

Makaton is a communication programme based around a core vocabulary, using speech, signs and/or symbols. The Makaton Core Vocabulary was designed to be a small vocabulary of concepts enabling children and adults to better understand spoken communication, as well as develop useful communication with others!! In New Zealand the signs used with Makaton are from New Zealand Sign Language (NZSL) - the natural language of the deaf community in New Zealand. When signs are used with Makaton they are used in the order of spoken English to enable us to sign and speak at the same time.

The symbols have been especially designed for Makaton. Combining signs and/or symbols with speech has been shown to be very effective for many children and adults. Makaton is used widely in New Zealand with a wide age-range from pre-schoolers through to adults. It is used by parents and carers, teachers, speech language therapists and many others. (http://www.makaton.org.nz/about.htm)

Sign language has its own grammatical structure and uses combinations of hand movements, body movements and facial expressions. There are people who are first language sign and those who learn sign as a second or other language. Signs can be learnt alongside songs/music as well as through formal signing lessons. There is also a simplified sign language, which used to be known as Makaton. The SingingHandsUK YouTube Channel has a range of "carpark karaoke" songs that you can sign along to.

Each country has their own sign language, with Australian sign (or Auslan) being different to American Sign Language, British Sign Language and New Zealand Sign Language. NZ sign reflects both Maori and non-Maori concepts and culture. The image on the next page shows the signs for the letters of the alphabet.

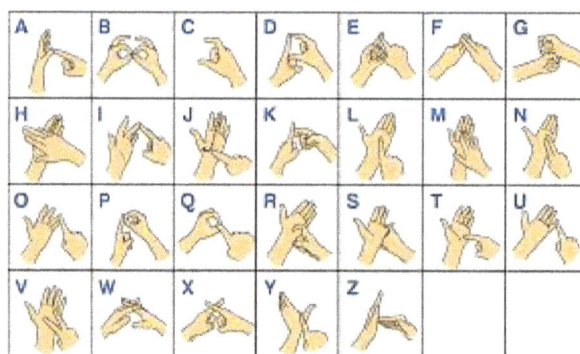

Auslan Fingerspelling

Most sign languages have an office website and a range of informal resources can be found on-line; for example, Facebook, Instagram and YouTube.

Picture Exchange Communication System (PECS) and other visuals

Firstly, it is important to note that the use of PECs or other visuals as the main form of communication will not prevent speech from developing, if anything it is likely to support the child in learning to speak if they have this potential. PECS is a system of communication that uses particular symbols (physical pictures) and follows a particular format. PECS starts off by teaching students to give a picture of a desired item to an adult, who immediately fulfils the request. For example, if the child wants a drink, they will give a picture of 'drink' to an adult who directly hands them a drink. When using PECS verbal prompts are not used as they are creating prompt dependency.

Over time PECS teaches many symbols and how to construct simple sentences or questions with these symbols. PECS is used around the world with both adults and children. PECS is a

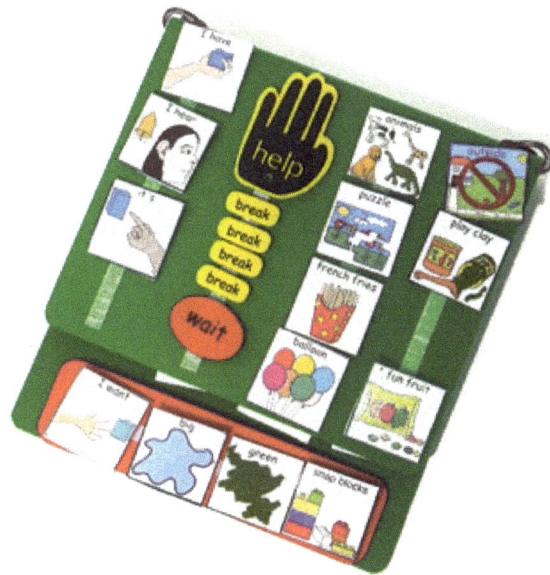

PECs Boards
pecsaustralia.com

paper format system and students require large spiral bound communication books which store the symbols. PECS is a visual communication tool which uses pictures, but there is a specific protocol for teaching expressive use of pictures for an individual to communicate wants and needs, and to comment about the world. There are apps for supporting PECS, but these are not designed to replace the hard copy communication boards.

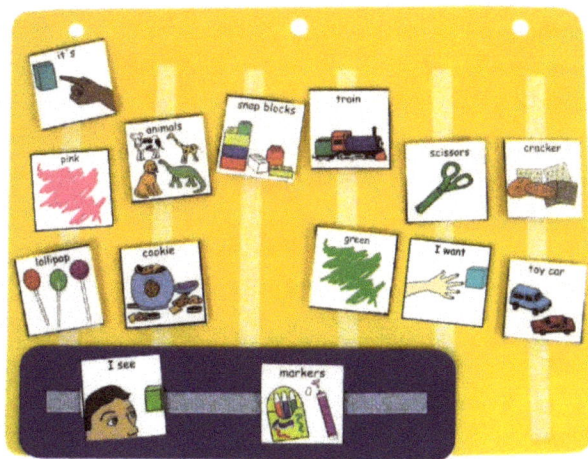

PECs board
pecsaustralia.com

The protocol involves 6 distinct phases of teaching, as well as strategies for introducing attributes (e.g. colour and size) into the individual's language. It combines knowledge from the fields of applied behaviour analysis and speech-language pathology to produce an effective and efficient method for teaching functional communication. To use PECS according to protocol you need to attend a PECS workshop. In New Zealand these are run by http://www.pecsaustralia.com/ .

Due to the cost of all the materials some people choose to use their own modified system, or to use electronic systems, for example apps on iPads. Proloquo2go is one of the most popular electronic system which can be combined with hard copies often called PODS.

Spoken Language

Spoken language communication can be made much easier and more effective when adults use language that suits the autistic spectrum style of language. This is because people who are on the autistic spectrum are highly logical, we use logic to interpret not only our environment, but the way people interact with us. Rules are one aspect of our logical thinking. We can use rules in the same way as non-autistic people, for example saying thank-you whenever someone gives us a gift. However, we also use rules to guide us in most social situations. Sometimes, we have misunderstood or interpreted things and so develop a rule that is fundamentally flawed. For example, we may have a rule that says, 'when people say how are you, you say fine thank-you', which sounds fine.... However, we may apply this rule when injured and so instead of informing someone of an injury or hurt, we may say, "fine thank-you" when asked how we are. If the query had been, 'where are you hurt?' it would have avoided the resultant miscommunication.

Whenever oral communication and autism are mentioned together the speaker is usually launching into a short explanation of the perceived shortcomings around language for those on the spectrum. However, I would and do argue that autistics often have a better grasp of grammar, syntax and language than many others. I would also argue that a fluid spoken language ability is more to do with sensory and/or emotional overload than a lack of language skills as evidenced by the beautiful and highly-skilled writings, both fiction and non-fiction of some well-known non-speaking autistic adults. I would suggest that an autistic child who makes movies with a passion and skill not evident in their spoken language is communicating with skill and passion in their chosen way. Non-autistic film directors are certainly accepted as communicating via their movies, so why not autistics.

Spoken language is both more important and less important to myself and others on the spectrum. More important in that we value words, treasure their meanings, their shape, texture and sound, and less important in that we value and appreciate silence between words, are comfortable with communication being in other formats such as sign, type, emotion, or body movements.

I do not believe that the majority of people understand that they often say one thing and mean another in such a casual manner. I think this is because most people do not find anything of value in their own words. Why would one adult say to another, "I'll phone you later," and then not do so. When I talk with my allistic colleagues or friends, they suggest various reasons for saying this and then not following through with an actual phone call.

These reasons are listed below:

1. The person talking doesn't want to meet the other person again, but it rude to say this. When the other person doesn't get a phone call, they know that the talker is not interested in meeting up again. (Autistic response in my head, what the???? If you don't want to meet someone again say thanks for the evening/meal/whatever and leave)

2. The person talking is demonstrating a continued interest in the other person in a socially con-

ventional manner, i.e. saying they will talk to them later. Autistic response in my head, but how do you know it is not wanting to meet again or continued interest? This is very confusing.

3. This is just a casual comment/statement like 'see you tomorrow' it means I may or may not call/see you tomorrow, but I am fine with doing so. This may or may not contain emotional feelings within it. Autistic thoughts in my head.... Ok so this is basically a social construction with a number of different possible meanings that I may or may not understand.

This is why an autistic would say to another person, "I'll phone you later," and then not do so: they either became severely incapacitated or their phone did!

Another situation where oral language is used to mis-communicate by allistics is when leaving a social gathering early. Excuses are provided to the host along the lines of, 'my dog/child/work/sick relative require my presence. As I understand it, this is so that the host is not offended by a guest leaving early. I wonder what happens if there really is a sick relative at home/in the hospital? How does one know the difference?

This is what an Autistic would say before leaving a social gathering, "thanks for inviting me, I am tired now and need to go home". I am unsure why someone could be offended by this. It says what it means.

And that I think is one of the fundamental differences in spoken language use by autistics versus allistics. We say what we mean and consciously mean what we say, whereas allistics are constrained by a social code around spoken language use that does not prioritise meanings of words. Instead words are vehicles to convey social attitudes and hidden agendas, not to communicate clearly at all. This is not the same in all spoken languages or cultures, i.e. Dutch in the Netherlands, where the majority of people say what they mean and mean what they say. However, the English language and those cultures that speak it seem to prioritise tact, social attitudes and hidden agendas most of the time.

I am ever grateful to my primary school in Cumbria, in the UK, for explicitly teaching us the hidden agenda behind words in that culture. We started by looking at houses being advertised for sale. Close to transport turned out to the favourite euphemism for train/highway right next to the property. Perfect for DIY enthusiasts translates as falling down property and so on. We went on to study advertising, oral selling techniques, political speeches and so on. This mean that I understood from the age of 8 or 9 that people can and do use language to deliberately miscommunicate. However, I still find it jarring that ordinary people in ordinary situations feel the need to hide their true meanings in oral language that says one thing and means another. Why? What is the point? Isn't it more hurtful to wait hours or days for a phone call than to be told, thanks but no thanks?

Autistic children and students at school rarely get explicitly taught about deliberate miscommunication in oral language, and if they do, not usually until high school. The problem with this is that instead these children learn that their teachers lie and/or are stupid. For example, students are often told 'in 5 minutes' x will happen. Ten or more minutes go by and x has still not happened. The autistic student who can tell the time has two choices of thought in these cases, either the teacher can't tell the time (in which case they are stupid) or the teacher didn't mean it in the first place (in which case they are a liar). I don't think that either of these thoughts are helpful for long-term student teacher relationships. However, when I discuss this with colleagues, they either don't believe me, or they say that the students need to learn that they as teacher are meaning in around five minutes if nothing else more important comes up.... My response as an Autistic and an educator is, "Say that, say exactly what you mean and mean exactly what you say."

Thank-you to the teachers who have gone on to change the way they talk so that ALL their students, especially those on the spectrum whether diagnosed or undiagnosed, know not only what the teacher means, but go on to develop positive relationships with those teachers. These lucky students know their teachers are not stupid and do not mislead them constantly. Thank-you again.

When you interact with someone on the autistic spectrum, it is very important to always say what you mean and mean what you say. This applies equally to questions as statements. A generic question, 'how are you' is not saying what you mean, if you are meaning to elicit information about whether or not someone is hurt or injured.

In addition, most of us on the spectrum, although we can be quite argumentative and talk incessantly (or talk very little, if at all), we may not actually take in all the words within the wordy statements or questions of others. There are a couple of reasons for this which vary from person to person. Some autistics are slow processing spoken words, some have sequencing difficulties, some will be distracted by other sensory input. Additionally, if an autistic is emotionally or sensorially overloaded they will be less able to take in and understand what is being said to them. You may not be able to tell if this is the case for the person that you are talking to. It may be obvious if someone cannot/doesn't talk back to you, but this does not mean that they have nothing to say, just that you need to find out how they wish to communicate back with you.

If you are the parent/teacher of a child/young person on the autistic spectrum or the friend/partner of an adult on the spectrum, you may be asked or feel the need to interpret situations or events for that person from time to time. Adults and young people may ask for this input or they may not welcome it if given unasked. For younger children it is important that you support them to interpret events and conversations as others have meant them to be interpreted. This aides in the development of accurate and useful rules for the children to follow and may help prevent the application of rules in situations where they are inappropriate. For example, autistic children do not just know that you speak more quietly in some places than others, they need to be told. Another example is the type of words being used. Autistic children may not realise that the new word they heard in the playground is not appropriate as a name for their dog/teacher/teddy for example.

Autistic teens are finding their way in the world and have to learn that the intent behind some language is not the same as others. Other teens can tell by body language or tone of voice that someone has malicious intent, but autistic teens are unlikely to pick up on that. Parents, good friends and teachers can be invaluable in helping teens navigate their way as they learn about good friends and mean people pretending to be friends.

Just as an aside, I work with lots of kids on the spectrum with great senses of humour, and I share lots of laughs with other autistics online and in person. Our humour tends to be visual and/or word based for those of us who love words. However, we often do not understand many common jokes and either ignore them or laugh when other people laugh because we have learnt that we should laugh when everyone around us is laughing. Autistic children and teens benefit from finding others who share their sense of humour and being encouraged to use humour to diffuse tense situations in the playground and school, rather than aggression. This helps with confidence and schools like it!

Common communication issues with speech

"John" doesn't respond when I say his name.	John may not understand that you saying his name means you want his attention – say what you mean
Sarah doesn't answer social greetings appropriately	Sarah may not know that you want her to say hello back to you.
When I ask questions Tahu doesn't say anything	Tahu may need more time to process your question before responding. Allow 30 seconds for a response, then rephrase question more clearly

Summary main points – communication strategies

1. Say what you mean, mean what you say

2. Use clear and logical language, avoiding jargon.

3. Do not talk just for the sake of talking, keep to the point and then wait for a response.

4. If we are slow processors of words, please only ask one question at a time. Only give one instruction and wait until it has been followed to give the next instruction.

5. Do not expect an understanding of body language or tone of voice. For example, just because you raise your voice when you are angry does not mean the child/young person knows that is what you mean. It is better to say, "I am angry now."

6. Clarify that the child/young person has understood what you think you have said/asked.

7. Do not get angry when told NO, after asking, "would you do x, y or z?" No is a legitimate response to a would you question! If it is an order not a real question, phrase it as such by saying what you mean and meaning what you say.

8. Be aware that distracting things in the environment may receive more attention than your voice, unless you gain the child/young person's attention first. Autistic people do not automatically prioritise speech over other sensory input, nor do we automatically prioritise people over other things.

9. Your emotional response may not be the same as an autistic person's emotional response. You would not expect your friends to all have the same emotional reactions that you do, it is ok for an autistic person to have a different response too. If you find a response offensive, say so calmly and politely. For example, "it is rude to laugh when someone says they lost their job. Please don't do this, it makes people angry."

10. If you don't like something said or done by a child/young person on the spectrum, be clear about what you don't like and why. Express this in two short sentences, no more.

11

⚜

Social skills versus etiquette

Social skills are the skills needed to participate effectively in interpersonal situations, that is to say all situations that involve more than one person. Our world is a highly social world, and this is evident in education and work, where people are expected to collaborate and work alongside others. For people who are naturally social, social skills are picked up as they grow up. It is more difficult for children on the autistic spectrum, as they need to actively learn social skills.

Etiquette is the part of social skills that encompasses good manners. Manners are socio-cultural in origin and vary across nations. However, within that range, there are a few things that are deemed good manners/etiquette around the world, such as please and thank-you. Even for children that really struggle to learn social skills, learning to use please and thank-you is quite easy. This is the case, whether the child is using verbal language or sign.

Although both social skills and etiquette are niceties rather than necessities, they make a huge difference in the way other people view children. An autistic child that starts school able to use please and thank-you appropriately is usually more acceptable to their teachers than one that doesn't. Social skills will take many years to learn as they are complex and vary according to a range of things that autistics find baffling, like social status of the person being interacted with.

To teach please and thank-you, ensure these are modelled consistently (used by you in the child's presence). For example, saying or signing "Please clean your teeth," and following this up with "Thank-you for cleaning your teeth," once your child has complied. Explain to your child that saying please when they are asking for something makes other people happier to comply and is a good thing to do. When you give your child anything, teach them to say or sign thank-you as they receive it. Praise them initially for using please and thank-you, being very explicit in the praise. For example, "Great thank-you Sarah, I like it when you say thank-you." Then slowly move to intermittent praise, praising less and less frequently, but with the same enthusiasm. Intermittent positive feedback has been shown to be more effective than constant praise.

Learning please and thank-you does not require a high level of oral language skill and can be used alongside one and two-word phrases, such as please juice, please music, thank-you toast. The use of please and thank-you will become habitual over time. Your child may need support to generalise the use of please and thank-you to situations outside the home, such as the shop, with family and the wider community. This would ensure that by the time they start school, your child automatically says please when requesting things and thank-you when receiving things.

The issue of social skills is much more complex, as it involves everything from conversations in the playground to how to behave at a party. There is a range of sociability within the autistic spectrum, but even for the most social of autistics, social situations are tiring and require a huge amount of energy and concentration to interpret and respond. Most allistic children relax at playtime, having a break from learning by interacting with their peers. For autistic children the playground is not relaxing, and they often try to retreat to quiet spaces to avoid socialising.

Understandably it can be difficult to ascertain if an autistic child wants to be by themselves because they like to be alone, or if it is because they need to learn the skills to be around others. However, trying to teach an autistic child to be as social as their peers is pointless, for schools or families. Autistic adults can work in social environments, but nearly all require alone time to relax and self-calm. It is unrealistic therefore to expect autistic children to be interacting with peers all day at school. Explicitly teaching conversational skills and a few playground games will facilitate choice for the autistic student, they will be able to join in if they want to.

For pre-school and young school children, these skills should be taught as a whole class, so that the autistic children feel a sense of belonging and those allistic children who have not had the opportunity to learn how to converse and play with another child positively are also able to benefit from the lessons. There is an excellent book that has been successfully used in New Zealand classrooms; Super Skills - A Social Skills Group Program for Children with Asperger Syndrome, High-Functioning Autism and Related Challenges by J. Coucouvanis (2005). Although designed for children with Asperger's, it has been successfully used with autistic children with minimal spoken language skills and with whole classes in regular schools.

The benefit of the Coucouvanis programme is that the teacher doesn't have to do any planning as it is all laid out clearly in the book. The sessions are easily integrated into end of day circle time or morning mat time. However, should you wish to do something less formal the following are topics that will need to be covered for most autistic children:

1. Looking at people when being spoken to or speaking to – generally foreheads or noses are more comfortable that eyes for autistic people.
2. Greeting people – smiling and saying hello, tone and volume of voice also need covering.
3. Introducing self – what to say and how to say it.
4. Good manners in introductions and meetings – for example what how are you means and how to respond to this question, when it is appropriate to ask.
5. Asking for help – getting attention, waiting for a response, making request.
6. What do when help is refused or delayed.
7. Asking to play with someone – playground games may need to be taught at the same time alongside this skill.
8. What to do when request to play is refused or delayed.

9. How to ask to be left alone politely.
10. Turn taking for games and conversations.
11. Recognising and responding to clear signals of annoyance/anger/boredom from peers.

More advanced topics would include conversation starters for different situations, recognising, interpreting and appropriately responding to a wider range of emotions in self and others.

Many autistic adults and young people report that they were bullying all the way through school, though there were more reports of consistent bullying in high school than primary school. Bullying is unacceptable in any circumstance, but where children are unable to express themselves clearly, as with many autistic children, bullying often goes unreported or unnoticed. Another scenario is often present whereby children are behaving in a bullying manner towards the autistic child, who does not understand that this is bullying and therefore accepts the behaviour as typical human interactions.

These autistic children often think that any interaction with others means that others are being nice to them. When this happen the children on the autism spectrum are often asked to do stupid, dangerous or bad things which their 'friends' find hysterically funny. When the autistic spectrum child gets into trouble, their 'friends' do not, and so think it is even funnier. At five the consequences may seem minimal, but at fifteen the consequences can result in criminal convictions and exclusion from school for the young Autistic.

This is why it is important for teachers and schools to foster a sense of community, where those who do not intervene to stop bullying are held as culpable as those who are actively bullying. Students should be explicitly taught about good/kind and bad/mean behaviour and how to identify if someone is truly being kind or is in fact being mean. The most important thing for any autistic is to feel comfortable in themselves, around other people.

For autistics there are a couple of differences in social behaviours that tend to be gendered. However, individuals may not present in the following ways:

GIRLS:

- Use media and observed situations to watch and take on board 'expected' behaviours enabling them to seem socially skilled by using sets of rules
- Will 'mask' their identity by mimicking others around them to fit in
- Prefer to instigate and control games rather than join in, but are able to join in

BOYS:

- Do not seem to 'learn' from media and observed situations, need explicit teaching for social skills
- (Computer violence in playground)

- Can be side-lined repeatedly due to lack of understanding of unwritten rules

12

❧

The roles and expressions of emotions and empathy in autism

What is empathy? The free online dictionary takes the 2003 Collins English dictionary definition that empathy in relation to other people is: "the power of understanding and imaginatively entering into another person's feelings" http://www.thefreedictionary.com/empathy

* * *

It used to be widely thought that autistics are unable to have or express empathy. More recently people with lived experience are being listened to more carefully about this emotional attribute. Whereas it had been thought that we had no empathy, this idea was based either on flawed psychology experiments or a misunderstanding of the experiences and expressions of autistics. Experiments were of the 'Sally-Anne doll type'. In this type of test, after introducing two dolls, the child/adult is asked a control question which is: 'what are the names of the dolls?'. A short skit is then enacted; Sally takes an object and hides it in her bag. She then exits the room and the. Child/adult is told Sally has gone for a walk. While she is away, Anne takes the object out of Sally's bag and puts it in her own bag. Sally is then re-introduced, and the child is asked the key question: "Where will Sally look for her object?" Technically this is a theory of mind test, looking at if the child/adult can understand or imagine what the doll Sally is thinking. However, the results, in which most autistic children said that Sally would look in Anne's bag, have been taken as showing that not only do autistics not have the ability to perceive things from another's point of view but their ability to understand emotions and respond to them is limited.

My issue with the Sally-Anne test is that the person undertaking the test is not told explicitly that Sally does not know what Anne is doing. I think that this is an important point because the experimenter is wanting the person to ascribe thoughts to an inanimate object that cannot think. If the experimenter is asking this, then how is one to know whether or not Sally can 'know' what Anne has done. Non-autistic children generally say that Sally thinks the object will be in her own bag, but they are more likely to be familiar with playing games that one second ascribe human or superhuman characteristics to inanimate objects and the next second do not. I think this is instead a classic demonstration of the hidden rules of non-autistic (allistic) interactions.

Leaving that aside and looking at the misunderstanding of autistic experience and expression, it is important to note that many allistics misread the emotions of autistics. I can be in a room with another autistic and just know how they are feeling, whereas the allistic teacher does not. Most adults on the spectrum indicate that they have had this experience frequently, and I think to is because our body language is often different to that of allistics. Many autistics have less expressive faces and more expressive muscle tone than allistics. Many, but not all of us seem to feel not only our own, but others' emotions, far more intensely than allistics. This intense experience combined with our atypical expression of this experience has led others to suggest we do not understand the feelings of others. An example of a common atypical expression of experience relates to the death of someone who has been ill for a long period of time. I, alongside many autistics have a gut reaction to this, which is a thankfulness that the dead person is no longer suffering. Psychologists have suggested to me, that my response is a compartmentalizing of experience, but I do not agree. I am also a Buddhist and my faith does not see death as negative, more a release from the suffering of this life and a gateway to the next life. I digress, back to empathy.

I am MORE profoundly affected by the release from suffering than by the sadness of those who are grieving. I do know that the people grieving are sad and yet, my Autistic logic keeps kicking in, telling me that all of these other people must have known the person was going to die, after all, we all die, especially once we have been ill a long time, and therefore even though they are sad, they must feel some sense of relief. I know from experience that this is not the case! But I cannot change that my prominent response is to the longer-term suffering having finally ended.

Another atypical expression, is that our responses to intense emotion (again our own or that of others) can be delayed by minutes, hours or days. We have the understanding of the other person's feelings, but the effects so intense that we cannot process a response quickly. I have learnt a number of responses to a range of situations and can appear to have appropriate timely responses, but in reality, my actual response is likely to happen a few hours later.

Most of the autistics I know are extremely kind and caring and are able to express their thoughts and feelings and responses to others, whilst demonstrating understanding of others, in writing. In person we can seem a little stand-offish, but this is usually because we are processing. However, our empathy can be tempered with our often-different system of prioritising. As with my priority of emotion following the death of a person who had been ill for a long time, we often analyse situations, and this see them from several points of view. For example, in a classroom, if a child (Jo) cries because another child (Bob) had taken their lunch, an autistic child may think any or all of the following:

- Taking others things is wrong, I must tell the teacher, they will make it better
- Jo will be hungry now, I could give them my lunch
- Bob must have not had any lunch of their own
- I could get the stolen lunch back because I saw where Bob put it

- Why are children so mean to each other?
- Jo looks really sad now

Their response will depend on which response they prioritised or processed first.... But their facial expression may not reflect their emotional state or expression. They may wail and howl or run off or do nothing, and their reaction can be and sadly often is, misunderstood.

Autistic adults modify their reactions in public, where excitement for others could naturally be demonstrated by hand flapping or twirling, they make look uninterested, but from experience know that flapping and twirling are misunderstood and unappreciated by others, when really, they are often a sharing of joy. Children on the spectrum may have not yet realised that others do not understand the way they communicate emotions. When you are supporting children on the spectrum to learn emotions, it helps to have an understanding of our own thought processes so that we learn to communicate effectively in this complex area.

An as Autistic, I get annoyed every time an expert says either that I have no empathy or that I am not capable of empathy. I don't know one person on the autistic spectrum that does not experience empathy in one way or another, especially in relation to others being bullied, teased or just plain not valued. I suspect that researchers, psychologists etc have come to the erroneous conclusion that we do not experience empathy because the autistic expression of empathy is atypical. However, when an autistic does not yet have interoceptive awareness, they are not yet able to 'feel' their feelings and emotions. If a child has never 'felt' sad, how do they know that sad is a not so pleasant emotion? You can only 'feel' feelings and emotions once you have the interoceptive awareness of your internal body state; illustrated by the lion in the image below.

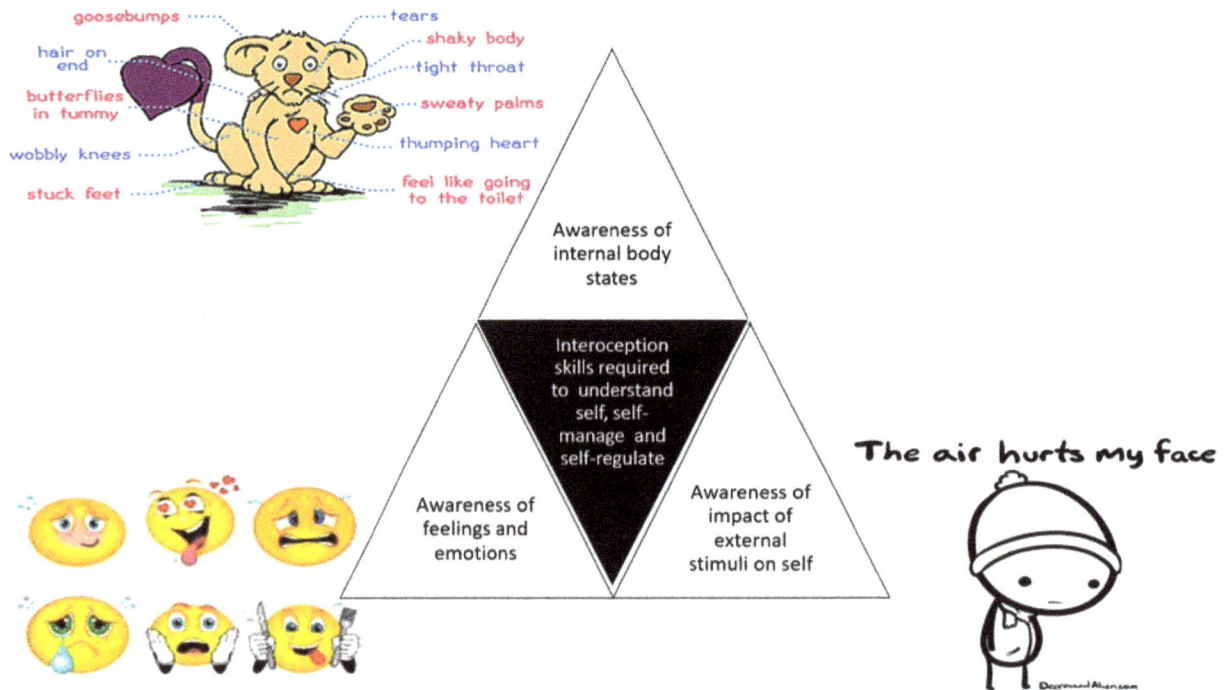

The three aspects of interoception required for self-regulation
Emma Goodall 2015

If I do not know what it 'feels like' to be sad, I cannot know how to respond appropriately. If I am told how to respond, it is a learnt response and not a truly empathic response. However, with the development of interoception, autistics do start to develop awareness of their own feelings and emotions and so can respond to the feelings and emotions of others with more understanding. For more information on interoception have a look online including at https://mindfulbodyawareness.com or the Healthy Possibilities YouTube Channel.

The concept of empathy is actually ascribed to two different things; the intellectual identification with the thoughts or feelings of another and then the different experience of – the actual experiencing of thoughts or feelings that another is having. Intellectual identification is the most common empathy experienced and expressed by autistics whereas I suspect that allistic people may actually experience the feelings of another, they certainly are observed to express themselves in a way that indicates this is the case.

An example – Ms A is in a singing competition and loses in the semi-final because she lost her voice. Ms A cries and says thing like, "I am devastated, I can't believe this happened."

An Autistic response would most likely be something like this: Ms A must be devastated; it can be really disappointing not to achieve something you really want. If pushed to discuss the situation further, an Autistic response would become even more of an intellectual identification, e.g., "it is however a competition, and you can't win a singing competition if you are unable to sing."

As I understand it, an allistic response would be more emotive, as evidenced by the crying of fellow competitors, who may actually be experiencing the same thoughts and emotions as Ms A, "how devastating to lose, what an awful time to lose her/my voice, I can't believe this happened."

To an observer behind a sound proof screen, the only evidence of empathy will be in terms of the second meaning, the actual experiencing of the thoughts or feelings as evidenced through body language. It is not possible to observe intellectual identification, but it does not mean that it does not exist or that it is not equally valid.

In addition, the autistic style of empathy is extremely useful in emergency situations, or in disasters. Instead of being overcome with emotions, following on from intellectual identification, autistics are highly likely to then continue along their intellectual thought path to think about what they can logically do to alleviate the situation.

This leads me to sympathy, which I think may actually be more of a difficulty for autistics that empathy, because there is no rational use for sympathy, although the dictionary suggested the act of sympathy is powerful and/or harmonious for the person being sympathized with and the sympathizer. Sympathy is the agreement in feelings between two or more people, more usually understood to be the expression of that agreement. This implies that sympathy is the expression of empathy, but only in instances where that empathy is the actual experiencing of the feelings of another.

Even if an autistic is sad at the same time as another person and because of the same thing, they are less likely to express that. Because many of us are very sensitive to the emotions of others and have an intense need for social justice at the same time as an abhorrence of suffering, if we sense another is very sad, we are more likely to change things than express empathy or sympathy. I don't know if this is because we identify more with a need for social justice or because by the time, we are adults we have learnt that most people do not appreciate the way we respond to their extreme distress.

Interestingly many autistics work in people orientated professions and seem to have some similar experiences. For example, people tell me their life story within a short time of meeting me. People ask me for advice around relationships and careers. I have since discovered that this is because I, like many autistics listen to what people say to us and rarely respond with anything other than logical responses of the; 'let's look at the pros and cons and then make a decision' type.

When a child falls over in the playground and cries, I check for injuries and if there are no visible injuries suggest that it will hurt for five minutes and then be better. This is usually true and always effective at ending the tears. I have seen my allistic colleagues provide far more empathy and/or sympathy and the tears take half an hour to subside. It is not that I don't understand the child is crying because they fell over, it is just that I know there is nothing that will hurt for long and that if I say this, the child will go off and play, get distracted and forget they had fallen and hurt themselves.

I identify myself as a kind and compassionate person, as do most of the adult autistics I know. None of us is particularly good at expressing the culturally appropriate responses of sympathy, but we are all capable of intellectually empathizing with others and working to help others live the best lives they can in that moment or in the long term. If autistics stopped being labelled as un-empathetic then maybe our type of empathy can be accepted and valued by the majority and not just those who know us very well personally.

If you want to help your child to develop an awareness of emotions and feelings, it is important to develop their interoception first and not start with labelling of emoticons. When I was required to teach emotion recognition via the use of emoticons, the students and I would pass the time guessing the emotions being presented as we often had no idea. You can observe/discuss with your child to ascertain their levels and domains of interoceptive awareness using the checklist on the next page.

13

Interoception checklist and strategies

BODY AWARENESS (Interoception)	Date observed	Observations/ indicators	Strategies which are helpful
Can feel their muscles tense and relax			
Can feel when they are cold			
Can feel when they are hot			
Knows when they are thirsty			
Knows when they are hungry			
Knows when they need to go to the toilet			
Knows when they are in pain			
Knows where it hurts when in pain			
Knows when they feel unwell			
Knows when they are starting to get upset			
Knows when they are starting to get anxious			
Knows when they are starting to get frustrated			
Knows when they are starting to get bored			
Knows when they are starting to get angry			
Knows when they are getting over excited			

Knows when they are getting overwhelmed			
Knows when they are tired			
Knows when they are happy			
Knows when they are calm			

This checklist was originally created By Emma Goodall and Michelle McAuley (2017) for DECD in South Australia and is creative commons licensed.

14

❧

Friends

Friends
(Natalia & Gabriel, 2006)

Artists tend not to paint in crowded rooms; poets rarely write their best work during parties, autistics rarely do their best work in group situations. This is because people on the autism spectrum think logically, they like to plan and structure pretty much everything and group work situations are rarely structured. In addition, social skills are not logical (for example, tact is in fact lying). As mentioned before, social situations are usually anxiety provoking for autistic children and adults, but conversely people on the autism spectrum usually do want to have friends and time to share their interests with others.

However, what friends are and what the concept conveys can be quite different for allistics and autistics. Friends are at a minimum level, people who share interests/time together because they want to. Other definitions include social/emotional expectations such as 'being there when your friend needs support'. Both adults and children on the autism spectrum may or may not place importance on these social expectations. They may however place expectations on things like having phone calls returned. If a person on the autism spectrum does not 'feel' liked or respected by the other person, they are unlikely to interact positively (or at all in many cases). Some people on the autism spectrum are 'super sensitive' to the emotions of others or places.

This heightened sensitivity can lead to an autistic child crying because others are crying or being extremely distressed when witnessing situations of unfairness or unkindness. These reactions are not melodramatic, they are a valid expression of what the child is experiencing. A useful technique for helping the child to manage this is to say, "go and get a drink of water. By the time you get back to class, you will feel better." The act of walking and focusing on getting a drink acts as both distractor and calmer, so the child does indeed feel better upon return. This is less successful with children who are accompanied by an adult. Teaching mindful body awareness (interoception) also helps autistics to self-manage and self-regulate.

Supporting the development of friendships

Due to the difference in friendship experience and desire by autistics, it is important to support the development of friendships that will be both meaningful and beneficial to the child. Shared interests are the most likely basis for friendships among autistics of all ages. Where the interests of young autistics are not known, social contacts should be set up where the child has the ability to be alongside rather than interacting head on, should they choose to do so. An example of this is to set up Lego play.

In Lego play, a box of Lego is emptied onto the floor. A rule is given to all the children that they must share the Lego, no-one is to take more than x amount. X should be modelled by grabbing a pile and showing the children the pile and then the pile spread out. Children are then free to use the Lego however they want, making things alongside others or with others. Some children will require prompts to make things as the choice of making anything can be overwhelming for some children.

Families can provide opportunities for the development of friendships by setting up play dates that involve parallel play, like Lego, or special interest activities. Many autistic children have really enjoyed learning martial arts, and there are a number of young people who have achieve black belts in a martial art. Martial art give the child a place to be social without having to be sociable.

Additional activities that have been really enjoyed by many (but not all) on the autistic spectrum are music, drama, dance and art. However, it is important to note that what suits one autistic child will be an anathema to another. For example, there are autistics who love to play soccer and are quite successful, but others for whom this would provoke immense anxiety and distress.

Autistic children will not realise they are meant to do things to maintain friendships, so their teacher or parent will need to do this for them initially. Over time the child can be taught to text or even phone their friends and to reciprocate invitations. For example, when teaching autistic teenagers to invite friends over to play computer games a verbal or written script can be provided if the teen is texting their friend. If the teen is going to phone, following a verbal prompt may be too difficult and an adult should model all the steps first. These consist of dialling, asking for the person with whom you want to speak, leaving a message if they are not there, asking them over if they are. Asking them over involves negotiating a day and time, which can be difficult until the teen has had a lot of practise. Video modelling can be useful to teach not just this skill, but many others. However, video modelling does not work for all autistics, so if it doesn't seem to have had any effect after a couple of goes, give up!

Many autistic children are left out when it comes to birthday parties and other social events. In some ways this suits these children, but it causes their families huge distress and means that the children do not have the same opportunities to develop an awareness and understanding of a range of social events and activities. This can lead to difficulties later in life, so it is worth advocating for autistic children so they do get invited to events and are given the opportunity to attend for as much or little time as they are comfortable with.

Many autistic teens attend school and other social events and enjoy them for some time, but then want to withdraw as the socialness becomes overwhelming. Ensuring the teen has their laptop/ game player or a book to read means that they can sit to one side and self-regulate by immersing themselves in their game or book. Over the years, I have observed that other teens and young adults are comfortable with this kind of behaviour and quite respectful.

Social stories and/or modelling of social events can be powerful supports for autistic children to learn how to manage themselves in a range of new situations. For example, when an autistic child who likes Lego is invited to a wedding they can be guided through what is going to happen and how to respond by an adult using Lego people to represent the bride and groom as well as the guests. Photos of where the wedding and/or reception are going to be held should also be shown to the autistic child along with explanations of how long the ceremony and/or festivities will last. This sort of preparation can take hours, but has been reported to be extremely successful for both the child and their families.

Using Lego to plan for a wedding
Emma Goodall 2020

Some children are not able to understand wordy social stories and are better supported by more visual stories, such as those created with boardmaker or other visuals or even videos. These could be photo stories, cartoons or boardmaker social stories. An example is given below:

I will have a birthday party.

Children will come to my party. They will

say, "Happy Birthday" to me. They will

bring presents that I can open after

we eat birthday cake.

Visual 'birthday party' story
http://www.slatersoftware.com/birthday%20social%20story.pdf

15

Obtaining autistic engagement in learning

Obtaining engagement and compliance can be a big problem for parents /teachers of the logical autistic child, for two main reasons; the child can't do what is requested or the child won't comply. However, despite the appeal of compliance, it is dangerous to teach autistic children that they need to be 100% compliant. This is because complete compliance, combined with autistic difficulties with social communication, puts autistics at unacceptable levels of risk in terms of being taken advantage of by others.

Non-compliance, may not be with intent, it may be that the autistic is currently overwhelmed and unable to comply, or they may not have understood or even heard your request. In addition, they may be too anxious or stressed. A request to do something the child perceives as pointless/boring or stupid is not tempered by a social awareness or acceptance of the societal expectation that children do what adults request of them. Justifying and explaining your rationale or requests, if you use clear logical explanations will get you a long way. However, it is hugely helpful to work on the idea that some things just have to be done, regardless, as this will help the child succeed at school i.e. please & thank you, turn taking.

- Children will comply to make you happy if they think you like and value them.
- Conversely if they think you don't like them they won't do anything for you.

16

⁂

Strategies to diminish stress and anxiety

Decreasing stress and anxiety will decrease sympathetic nervous system overload (meltdowns/shutdowns)

Volcano erupting

SYMPATHETIC NERVOUS SYSTEM OVERLOAD: MELTDOWNS (externalising) SHUTDOWNS (internalising)	TANTRUMS
Uncontrollable Caused by overload and triggered by 'straw that broke the camel's back'	Controllable Caused by not getting own way Requires firm management and clear behavioural

| Requires time, space and sensory regulation to resolve | boundaries, don't forget at 16 there are legal implications for hurting others |

It is better to prevent sympathetic nervous system overload as the brain is not capable of defusing easily or quickly once SNS overload is in progress (no matter how the meltdown/shutdown manifests). Prevention is through sensory management, clear communication, facilitation of clear and accepted routines or self-control of environment, engagement in interoception activities and time to enjoy special interests. After the event, give the person time and space to self-regulate themselves (interoception activities are very useful for this for most people, in addition movement may help, whereas some individuals need silence and others a specific type of noise).

Sensory Sensitivities

Autistic people can be overly/hyper sensitive to sensory input or under/hypo sensitive to sensory input or a mixture of the two. This leads to both passive and active behavioural responses, illustrated in the diagram below. Sensory stimuli are any of the 8 senses:

- Tasting (including texture)
- Touch (including pressure)
- Noise (type and volume)
- Smell (type and intensity)
- Sight (objects, level of light & intensity of light, visual textures)
- Vestibular sensory experiences (balance/movement)
- Proprioception (sense of body in space)
- Interoception

SELF REGULATION

	PASSIVE	ACTIVE
HYPO (UNDER)	**Poor registration** Does not appear to notice sensory stimuli Responds slowly if at all	**Sensory seeking** Requires very high levels of sensory stimuli Actively creates or seeks sensory stimuli
HYPER (OVER)	**Sensory sensitivity** Highly distractibile with visual discomfort notice very low levels of sensory stimuli	**Sensory Avoiding** Actively avoids sensory stimuli Reduce sensory stimuli

(SENSITIVITY axis on left side)

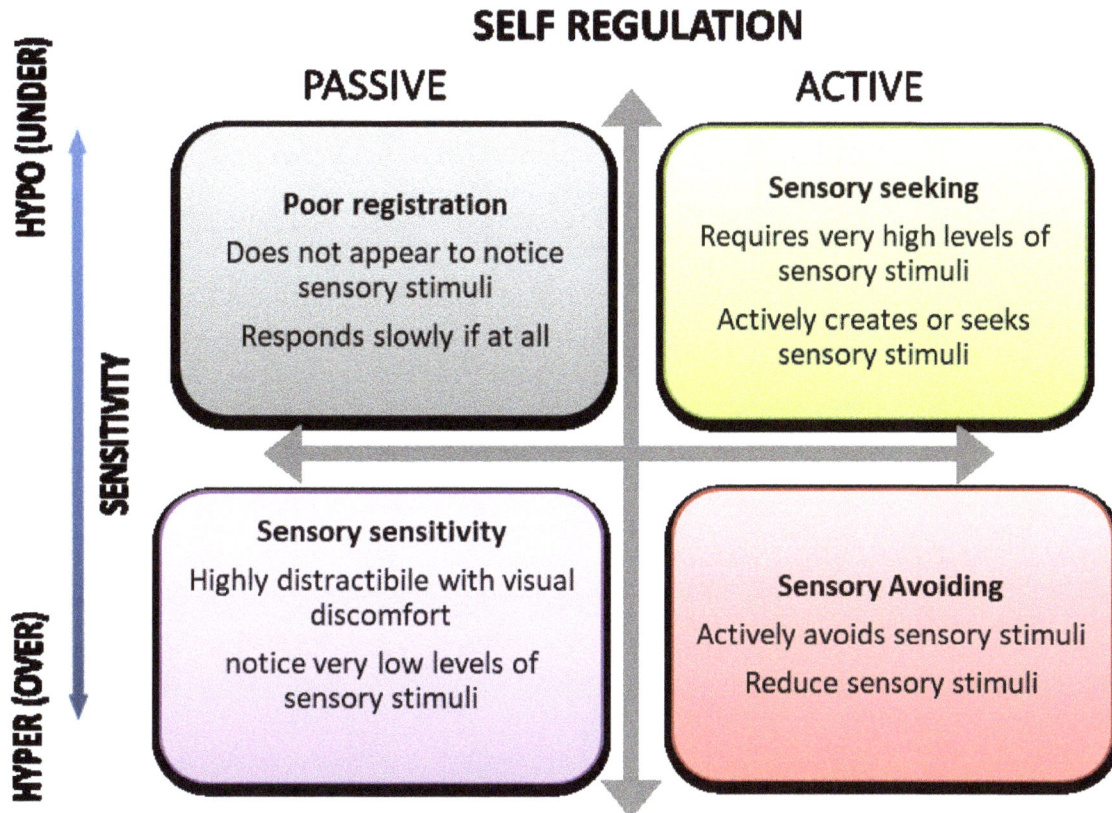

How individuals self-regulate interacts with their sensory sensitivities
Emma Goodall 2018

Autistic sensory differences are not static for life. Sensitivities are context dependent and can change from place to place or according to emotional and physical health. For example, if you are not particularly noise hyper-sensitive, you may be noise hyper-sensitive when you have a cold. Issues can present in a variety of ways, from putting hands over ears to sudden yelling and screaming or noticeable distress. Over time it is helpful to gain a deeper understanding of an individual's sensory profile and the strategies to use to prevent overload and maximize engagement in learning in school or relaxation at home. On the next few pages is a photocopiable sensory overview. If you would like a word-version visit: https://mindfulbodyawareness.com

To complete the sensory overview, it is helpful to meet as a team. The autistic individual may or may not want to attend a meeting but should always be part of the process, as their input is invaluable. One student was able to explain to his high school that he did not like the sound of paper, this was why he had done no written work for 2 years. If the school had known that when he started, they could have provided him with a laptop to do his work on, and given him the opportunity to wear headphones/listen to music to avoid the distress of hearing everyone else's paper!

SENSORY OVERVIEW

Student Name:
Date overview completed: Review Date:
Completed by:

BODY AWARENESS (Interoception)	√/x	Observation/explanation	Implication	Strategy to address or skills able to be applied in other areas
Able to name own emotions				
Able to recognise own emotions				
Knows when thirsty				
Knows when hungry				
Knows when they need to go to the toilet				
Able to say where hurts (accurately) when injured				
Knows when they feel unwell				
Knows when getting upset				
Gets distressed easily or frequently				
Knows when becoming anxious				
Gets anxious easily or frequently				
Knows when getting frustrated				
Knows when becoming angry				
Gets frustrated/angry easily				
Seems to react to the emotions of others/places				

VISUAL	√/x	Observation/explanation	Implication	Strategy to address or skills able to be applied in other areas
Does not recognise familiar people in unfamiliar clothes or unfamiliar contexts				
Dislikes bright lights				
Dislikes fluorescent lights				
Avoids bright light				
Attracted to lights				
Attracted to shiny objects and bright colours				
Attracted to patterns and visual textures				
Attracted to darkness				

SENSE OF BODY IN SPACE	√/x	Observation/explanation	Implication	Strategy to address or skills able to be applied in other areas
Does not seem to know where body is in space				
Gets lost in familiar places/routes				
Remembers routes and places				
Avoids escalators/travellators				
Dislikes crowds or being close to others				
Difficulties catching a ball				
Difficulties kicking a ball				
Appears not to see certain colours				
Walks into doors/people/objects				
Prefers to sit at back of group				
Prefers to sit at front of group				

AUDITORY	√/x	Observation/explanation	Implication	Strategy to address or skills able to be applied in other areas
Aversion to certain sounds				
Seeks or creates certain sounds				
Can hear sounds which others do not hear				
Bangs objects and doors				
Mumbles/talks/makes vocalisations to self constantly				
Changes vocalisations in reaction to environmental noises				
Changes vocalisations in reaction to emotional state				

AUDITORY PROCESSING	√/x	Observation/explanation	Implication	Strategy to address or skills able to be applied in other areas
Only seems to hear the first words of a sentence				
Can follow simple one step instructions				
Can follow complex or multi-step instructions				
Finds it easier to listen when not looking at person				
Echolalic (repeats phrases)				

TOUCH/TEXTURES	√/x	Observation/explanation	Implication	Strategy to address or skills able to be applied in other areas
Does not like shaking hands or being hugged				
Seeks/uses firm touch/deep pressure (incl. hitting)				
Seeks/uses light touch				
Aversion to certain fabrics/textures				
Attracted to certain fabrics/textures				
Very sensitive to pain and temperature				
Does not indicate sensitivity to pain or temperature				
Attracted to mouthing/chewing certain textures/things				
Avoids particular textures of food & drink				
Avoids particular colours/smells of food & drink				
Preference for food to not touch other food on plate				
KINAESTHETIC	√/x	Observation/explanation	Implication	Strategy to address or skills able to be applied in other areas
Tries to avoid using fine motor skills				
Enjoys using fine motor skills				
Difficulties with fine motor skills				
Tries to avoid running and/or climbing				
Enjoys running and/or climbing				
Difficulty running and/or climbing				
Tries to avoid riding a bike				
Enjoys riding a bike				
Difficulty riding a bike				
Poor balance				
Has extremely good balance				
Enjoys/seeks out swings				
Enjoys/seeks out trampolines				
Enjoys/seeks out slides				
Flaps hands when happy				
Flaps hands when anxious				

SMELL	√/x	Observation/explanation	Implication	Strategy to address or skills able to be applied in other areas
Avoids/dislikes certain everyday smells				
Attracted to certain smells				
OTHER	√/x	Observation/explanation	Implication	Strategy to address or skills able to be applied in other areas
Rocks when......				
	√/x	Observation/explanation	Implication	Strategy to address or skills able to be applied in other areas
ABLE TO SELF REGULATE UNAIDED				
At home				
In class				
In the yard				
Other				

How student presents	WHEN:	Where	PREFERRED STRATEGIES FOR SELF REGULATION
	happy	In classroom /yard/home/ community	
	calm	In classroom /yard/home/ community	
	angry	In classroom /yard/home /community	
	upset	In classroom /yard/home/ community	
	frustrated	In classroom /yard/home/ community	
	anxious	In classroom /yard/home/ community	
	Other – detail	In classroom /yard/home/ community	

Sensory Overload

When autistic children are exposed to sensory input that that find distressing or that they have an aversion to, they can quickly become overloaded. This means that emotionally/mentally they are unable to cope with the sensory input any longer. Overload often leads an autistic child to attempt to withdraw, and if they cannot avoid further aversive sensory input they will go into sympathetic nervous system (SNS) overload and a meltdown/shutdown will ensue.

Avoidance can be anything from running out of the room, to simply putting their hands over their eyes or ears. Understandably teachers are not happy with students running out of the room as it leads to health and safety concerns. To avoid this issue a student should be shown how to signal they are leaving the room because they need to, for example by turning over a card on the classroom door as they leave. In addition, the student should be shown where to go when they do need to leave the room. Regular interoception activities throughout the day can activate the parasympathetic nervous system, calming students and helping to prevent SNS overload.

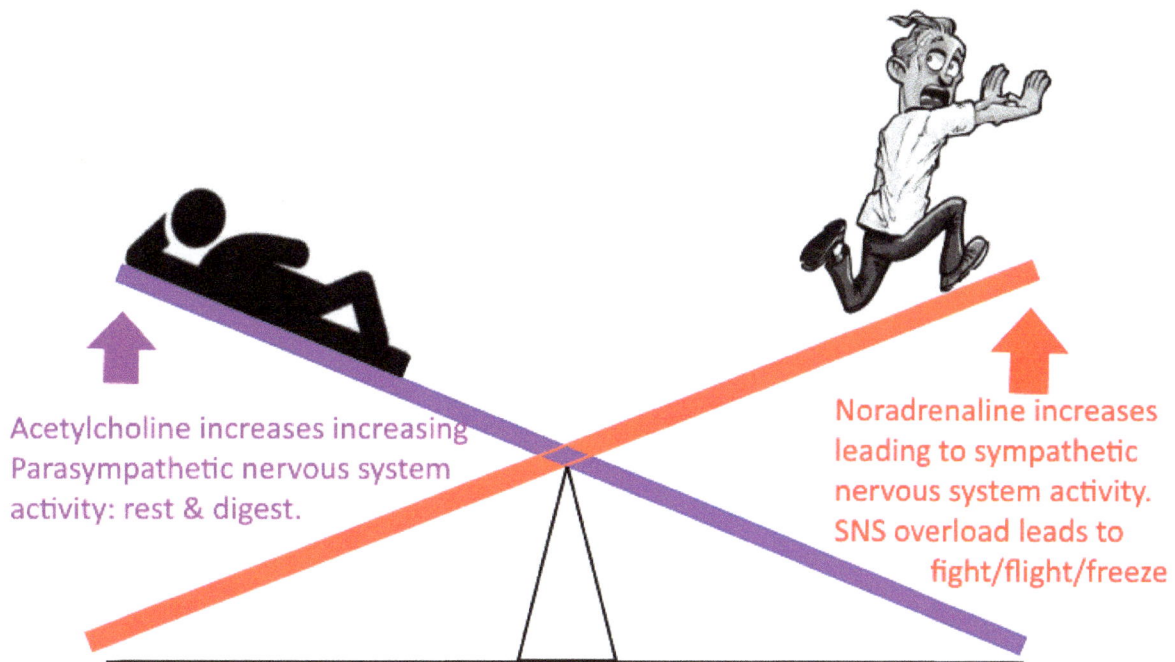

Acetylcholine increases increasing Parasympathetic nervous system activity: rest & digest.

Noradrenaline increases leading to sympathetic nervous system activity. SNS overload leads to fight/flight/freeze

The Autonomic Nervous System (ANS) can be represented by a seesaw
Emma Goodall 2015

A safe space/quiet space within school is very useful for autistic students (and students who have experienced trauma or have mental health difficulties). This can vary from school to school, but it needs to be a space that is always available to the child during school hours and does not require the use of extra adults, unless the space is also used by other students. Examples are; a special seat in the school office, a tent behind the teacher's desk (avoids child leaving room altogether), a den in the cloakroom or the school library, an interoception room.

Many autistic spectrum students initially find assembly overwhelming, and this is often assumed to be a noise issue, but it is not always about the noise. Although assemblies are often noisy, it can be the proximity to a very large group of other students that is difficult for the student. Headphones or earplugs/phones can be worn if it is purely a noise issue. If, however, it is related to the crowdedness of the hall, then the student should be allowed to enter the hall after all the other students and to sit at the edge near an exit until they feel comfortable moving closer to their class. They may always be more comfortable at the edge of a row, rather than in the middle and sitting at the very back or very front too.

Calming and Self-Calming Strategies

Sensory overload can be prevented by ensuring the autistic spectrum student is not subjected to any of the sensory inputs that they find aversive or difficult. However, this is not always practical or possible and so the child needs to be taught how to calm themselves down to either prevent or manage overload.

Using the sensory profile, it should be easy to see which sensory activities each particular autistic spectrum student really enjoys and seeks out. These are the sensory sensations that are positive for the child. Some of these will be pleasurable but not calming, so observations need to be undertaken of the autistic spectrum student engaging in their positive sensory activities. These observations aim to identify one of two activities that seem to result in the child becoming calmer – and these will be the preferred strategies for calming/self-regulation by that child.

For example, if a child likes to filter sand through their fingers repeatedly, but is visibly excited by this activity, filtering sand many not be suitable for self-calming. This same child is observed to become relaxed when they are rubbing the velvet paw of one of the classroom teddies. It is not practical for the child to carry the teddy everywhere 'in case they need it'. Next time the teacher observes the child starting to get overloaded, they could try giving the child a small piece of velvet to rub. If this works and is calming for the child, it could be a preferred strategy. Small pieces of velvet could be given to all adults who have contact with the child and they could have pieces in their desk, tote tray, bag, pocket etc. Preferred self-calming strategies are different for different autistic spectrum students. Here are some of the strategies that I have observed working for individual children:

- Going for a run around the edge of the playground three times
- Sitting in the reading corner, reading to self
- Rocking self
- Chewing a string necklace
- Swinging on the monkey bars
- Listening to particular music through headphones
- Squeezing a small ball
- Sitting in a large cardboard box (dark & quiet – had cushions on the floor)

Routines versus Control/Predictability

Fixations on routines are rarely about the 'need for routine' per se; rather they are a need for control over an intense world. Where the need for routine has become so entrenched that the child on the autism spectrum has a meltdown whenever the routine is changed, this causes lots of difficulties. In this case signal changes well in advance – both verbally and visually. Explain why the change is happening and what will happen next. Control/understanding is more important for other people than a need for routine. Routine is merely an easy way, for autistic spectrum children who are having difficulty with sequencing and the concept of time of day, to have an understanding of what is going to happen next. If at all possible, avoid a dependence on routine from occurring by varying things within the day from early infancy.

Routines can act as self-regulation and create an understandable world. They can be viewed as problematic by others who require flexibility (what is logic about flexibility – it is really only poor planning). Routines can also be used to acquire new skills and/or knowledge in a stress-free manner.

For example, if an autistic spectrum child always goes for a walk after lunch, this walk can be used to meet new people or see new things. Don't forget what routine for one person is not for another and is not required for another. Predictability is more important than routine, and where control is not possible, it is helpful to ensure autistic children and young people always know what is happening next, as this will help minimize anxiety and stress.

Fixated Thoughts – the pros and cons

It is well known that autism includes the character traits of repetitive actions/behaviours; however, this impacts life less than the trait of repetitive thoughts, otherwise known as fixated thoughts or the broken record way of thinking! Not all autistic thoughts are fixated; however, the ones that become fixated tend to become very problematic.

For example, when someone autistic decides that another person (i.e. teacher) does not like them and starts to fixate on this, they will rarely if ever change this thought, no matter what. So, this needs to be prevented at all costs, or you need to change classrooms or even schools! Prevent this with the first meeting between an autistic spectrum child and their new teacher being set up so the new teacher is calm, warm, respectful and considerate. If the teacher mentions your child's special interest, there will be an instant connection which can help to prevent negativity from the autistic spectrum student. This passion or interest should be used to introduce new topics and skills whenever possible, especially if the autistic spectrum student is otherwise minimally engaged in learning at school.

On the plus side, fixated thoughts that relate to special interests or learning can be great drivers to engage in tasks and develop skills and knowledge. For example, a fixation on fire trucks may lead an autistic child to develop the fitness and physical skills required to become a fire-fighter.

Summary main points – diminishing stress and anxiety

1. Autistic Spectrum students experience more stress and anxiety than other students.
2. Minimizing autistic spectrum student stress and anxiety will minimize meltdowns and help to promote wellbeing long term.
3. Create a sensory profile to help manage the environment and explore effective calming strategies.
4. Support student to regularly engage in self-calming strategies. This will minimize stress and anxiety and promote focus and availability to learn.
5. Until an autistic spectrum student can self-advocate it is the teacher's responsibility to manage the environment so that overload is minimized.
6. Routines are not mandatory.

7. Signalling what is going to happen is vital for the wellbeing of autistic spectrum students.
8. Changes and transitions need to be clearly signalled in advance (2-5 minutes before) and again when they are about to happen.
9. Changes need to be briefly and factually explained – x is not happening, instead we are going to do y.
10. Prevent negative fixated thoughts about yourself as teacher or about school by creating a bond with the autistic spectrum student the first time you meet them. Do this by being warm and welcoming and if possible talking about their special interest.

17

Strategies to Increase Confidence and Contentment

All people benefit from being content and confident in themselves, both in terms of mental health and self-esteem. Without self-confidence it is almost impossible to be content within one's self. For children on the spectrum, their risk of depression and/or anxiety is much higher than their peers and this needs to be counteracted by actively trying to build confidence and competence. By definition, children on the autistic spectrum struggle with social skills and managing interpersonal relationships. This difficulty is compounded by their lack of understanding of the hidden rules that govern social behaviour, both in and out of the classroom. These unspoken rules are often called the hidden curriculum. Autistic spectrum students will benefit from being specifically taught the hidden curriculum on a daily basis. This should be done both at home and at school. However, the impact of other people being accepting and seeing value in the autistic individual is known to have a higher impact on wellbeing than any other strategy, so peers need to be explicitly taught to be kind, respectful and considerate of each other to support the wellbeing of everyone in class.

Teaching the hidden curriculum

The hidden curriculum is huge, and between teachers and families it will still take years to cover all aspects of these unwritten and unspoken rules. However, even learning one rule, such as; 'people like it when you smile at them when you meet them,' can be very useful all through life. For autistic spectrum children, life can be very confusing, with people saying one thing but something different happening. Often the first activity of the day takes place in schools 'on the mat'; however, this rarely involves an actual mat. Instead 'mat time' takes place on an area of carpet or other flooring that has no desks on it! Where most of the class may take on board the idea of mat time, the spectrum child may be distracted looking for a mat!

Each non-literal phrase or sentence that is used frequently should be explained to the child, clearly and succinctly. For example, "when I say it is mat time we sit in this part of the classroom." Additionally, concepts like responding to the roll, putting your hand up to indicate you want to speak (and waiting until the teacher says your name before speaking), all need to be explicitly taught. Other non-classroom based social norms should also be explicitly taught, for example bathroom behaviours.

Examples of the hidden curriculum and teaching strategies

Hidden curriculum concept	Example of what needs to be taught
The roll	Sit quietly until the teacher calls your name, and then reply by saying.... Then sit quietly again.
Listening to the teacher	Do not talk to other children when the teacher is talking.
News	News does not mean new information; it is when you say something that you have done recently. If you have done something which you do not often do, this should be what you talk about.
Hold the door	Stand next to the door and hold it open for people to walk through.
Taking turns in a conversation	When you talk to someone, you need to take turns talking and listening. However, when the teacher gives the class instructions, this is not a conversation and you do not need to respond, unless you are asked to do so – then you have to!
Waiting for a turn on the playground climbing equipment	In the playground sometimes children push, however, no-one should push on the climbing equipment. If you want to go down the slide, you need to get to the top (not by going up the actual slide) and then wait behind the children who are at the top of the slide. Each child who is waiting will get a turn, the children who arrived after you need to wait until after you have been down the slide.
Class rules	There are class rules. Mostly you need to follow these all the time. The teacher does not like it when you tell them every time someone breaks a rule, but if the teacher asks who did something and you know, you should tell them quietly at the next break. If one of your peers tells you to do something and it is against the rules you may get into trouble.
Morning tea	This is the time when you have a drink and a snack (from your lunchbox) and then once your lunchbox has been put away you can play outside. If it is raining you will stay inside. There is no tea at morning tea. You need to wait until the teacher tells you to get your drink and snack. When the bell goes you must not just go to morning tea!

18

Presuming Competence

The single biggest block to a spectrum child achieving is the assumption that the child can't rather than that they can. Whether or not a spectrum child is able to talk when young does not mean the child can't learn and doesn't have potential to grow and develop. Some non-speaking children will learn to use PECS or communication devices, some will learn sign, some will develop speech and some a combination of things.

> *Perception drives expectation*
> *Expectation drives opportunity*
> *Opportunity drives achievement*
> *Achievement drives perception*

It can be difficult for adults to presume competence when a child's development is different to that of their peers. Even when a spectrum child is hyperlexic (teaches self to read before starting school), adults often assume the child does not understand what they are reading and that they are either just decoding text and/or have just memorised the words. Explaining things can be difficult for some on the spectrum, whereas others on the spectrum struggle with closed questions. Finding out the strengths and the struggles of individuals will not only help in planning for parenting strategies/teaching and learning but also in framing the spectrum child as a competent learner.

Goal setting

Having regular goal setting and evaluation meetings, for example termly individual education plan meetings, will enable everyone to see progress more readily. This is especially important if the autistic spectrum student is working at a substantially lower level or slower pace than their peers, as it is easy for a teacher to not see the progress when thinking about the class as a whole. Teachers are often quite surprised by the progress that autistic spectrum children do make over the time they are in a school, especially in terms of behaviour and academic output.

Even so, within a school year, these same teachers find it much harder to pinpoint progress and therefore to presume competence and so offer opportunities to further develop competence and confidence (Goodall, 2013). For example, in a class of five years olds there will be a huge variation in writing skills, which over the school year will all improve. However, the improvements may be far greater for some of the students than for an autistic spectrum student with a sensory aversion to paper, or a difficulty with fine motor skills that means it is difficult for them to hold and move a pencil. In this case, mid-year the teacher may not see that the autistic student has made progress because they are now able to write one or two words unaided, because the rest of the class can now write 2-10 sentences unaided.

Valuing Autistic Skills

An attention to detail, a tendency to perfectionism, a natural sense of justice and conception of the equality of living beings are just some of the positive aspects of autism. Some autistics are also very skilled at taking things apart and putting them back together again, others at painting/drawing/design. Some also have prodigious memories and are able to recite whole movies/plays/songs easily. Most autistic spectrum children are caring and kind, though they may not always know how to express this appropriately.

The more characteristics of any student that are valued, the better that student will feel about themselves. This is no different for autistic spectrum students. If an autistic spectrum student is really good at cleaning and organising the classroom, make sure to let them know that the class value their skills in this area. If another autistic spectrum student makes movies, encourage them to show others how to do this. Use the splinter skills of the autistic spectrum students to teach their peers those skills and to demonstrate that all students have a range of talents and challenges.

Valuing Autistic Expressions

In a group of autistic spectrum adults, one of the things that is often said is how nice it is to be in a place where expressing ourselves is fine. No-one is going to look strangely or comment negatively about an adult flapping, rocking or bouncing in an autistic spectrum gathering. However, in education autistic spectrum students are often told not to flap or rock or do any repetitive behaviours that 'look different' or 'look autistic'. There are powerful and distressing stories from autistic adults who were not allowed to flap their hands or rock at school.

If a behaviour is not harmful to the autistic spectrum student or anyone/thing else, then there is no justification for stopping the child doing that. Most children go on to learn that these behaviours are not accepted by classmates long before they enter the world of work and so are not disadvantaged by them. If behaviour is harmful to self/others then it must be curbed. However, in curbing one behaviour, another will take its place that may be even less acceptable, so it is important to first think about acceptable replacement behaviours that will have the same sensory and emotional value to the autistic spectrum student. For example, trying to replace running around with reading is not going to be successful! Replacing running around randomly with running a prescribed route may well be successful.

Many autistics express themselves through creativity and this should be valued even when it is quite different to the creative work of peers. This expression may be through music, drama, art, cartooning, movie making, baking etc. The result is not always as important as the process, and autistic students should be allowed the time to follow the process through and then given the choice of displaying/sharing the result if they would like to, rather than this being teacher choice.

An example of autistic expression is shown in the photographs below, taken during a phase of intense interest in the visual textures of things.

Visual textures
Emma Goodall 2013

The Benefit of Autistic Arrogance

Many children and adults on the autism spectrum or with a diagnosis of Asperger's are aware of their cognitive abilities and many have been assessed as gifted. Even without the assessment, many of these autistics are quite arrogant about their intelligence. Tony Attwood often talks about the idea that autistics' sense of self-worth can be wrapped up in their intellectual identity. This identification as highly intelligent can act as a protective factor when other people are not being inclusive or even worse are being negative or derogatory towards a child (or adult) on the autism spectrum.

Harnessed effectively, this arrogance can act as a motivating factor to achieve academically or in any given domain. Indeed, there are said to be large numbers of university professors with undiagnosed autism! When these children are struggling socially they seek solace and enjoyment in things that stimulate their mind, such as books, research online, learning new skills. These aspects can be used by schools positively to support achievement, learning and exploring new skills.

Unfortunately, sometimes when children on the autism spectrum express this arrogance, it can come across to others as being a put down of others or a boast, rather than a factual statement. It is most likely that the autistic student thinks they are being purely factual when they say that they are more intelligent than everyone else in the class. This can be particularly annoying, should that particular student rarely do any actual classwork! If this is the case, asking the student to work on topics of their choosing, but in depth and detail may help to demonstrate their learning, not only to you but school boards and inspectorates.

Medications

For some autistic spectrum students, their anxiety or co-occurring ADHD may affect them so much that the family have chosen to use medication to support their child's wellbeing. Autistic spectrum people are known to have atypical reactions to most medications, and either require tiny doses or huge doses. Schools can support the effective medical management by noting down mood or behavioural changes in the day, along with the time they occur. This is because some medications produce troughs and peaks of effectiveness which can be tweaked by changing the time of initial medication or introducing a top up dose.

Summary of Main points – increasing confidence and competence

1. View the autistic spectrum child as a capable learner with potential and provide opportunities for the child to learn and celebrate their learning.
2. Over time work out the strengths and difficulties for the child.
3. Teach new skills/knowledge using the autistic spectrum student's strengths or special interests.
4. Demonstrate that you value the autistic spectrum student as much as the other students and that they are a valued member of the class.
5. Teach the hidden curriculum explicitly.
6. At least once a term facilitate sessions where the autistic spectrum child teaches their peers something. This can be as simple as a new sign or as complex as a presentation on a topic or a whole class where the autistic spectrum student teaches the class how to do something.
7. Ensure the autistic spectrum student has a choice over whether or not their creative work is displayed publicly.

8. Let the autistic spectrum child express themselves through body movements or vocalisations.

9. Facilitate deeper learning by challenging students with Asperger's to use their intelligence.

10. Monitor medication effects and feedback the information to the family/physician.

19

Supporting Positive Behaviour

One of the reasons that parents and teachers can find children on the spectrum stressful is that the children's behaviours can be challenging at times. As with all children the goal is to support the development of positive behaviour at all times. However, adults need to be aware that sensory and/ or sympathetic nervous system (SNS) overload will often result in a meltdown/shutdown and this should not be interpreted as bad/challenging behaviour on the part of the child. With young children, it is the adult's responsibility to ensure the child is protected from sensory or SNS overload; or guided to calming strategies when overloaded.

There is a difference between SNS overload and tantrums, and spectrum children do exhibit both. If a child becomes too wound up/hyped during their tantrum, it can turn into SNS overload, so it is important to intervene in a tantrum quickly. Also, it is important to note, that like all other children, autistic spectrum children can be naughty! Many have a big sense of humour, though their humour may be a bit different from the norm. This sense of humour can get them into trouble as they get older if they are not guided around appropriate humour in different situations. The following table reviews the key differences between SNS overload and tantrums and the causes of these:

SNS overload	Tantrum
Cause not always easily identifiable as usually due to a build-up of things.	Usually caused by child not getting their own way.
Once started needs to run its course, cannot be interrupted or stopped.	Can be interrupted or stopped by firm boundaries
Requires time/space/calming strategies to recover from – recovery can take hours	Requires distraction to move on from

If you imagine SNS overload as an exploding volcano, it is no good trying to plug the crater of the volcano, as the lava would burst out from somewhere else until the pressure had been released. This is just what it is like for someone on the autistic spectrum. In general, a child should be left alone and given a wide berth if they in SNS overload. However, if the autistic spectrum child is harming themselves or others or damaging at this time, an adult (or two) need to intervene to ensure that others are safe and that the child is also safe.

Following SNS overload, it is important to support the child to become truly calm, in other words to activate the parasympathetic nervous system. An interoception activity done for 5 mins or so will achieve this. An interoception activity is one where the state of the body is changed in one way and the individual is guided to notice it. This could be a breathing activity or a muscle tension/relaxing activity. The following example is from Interoception 101.pdf available online.

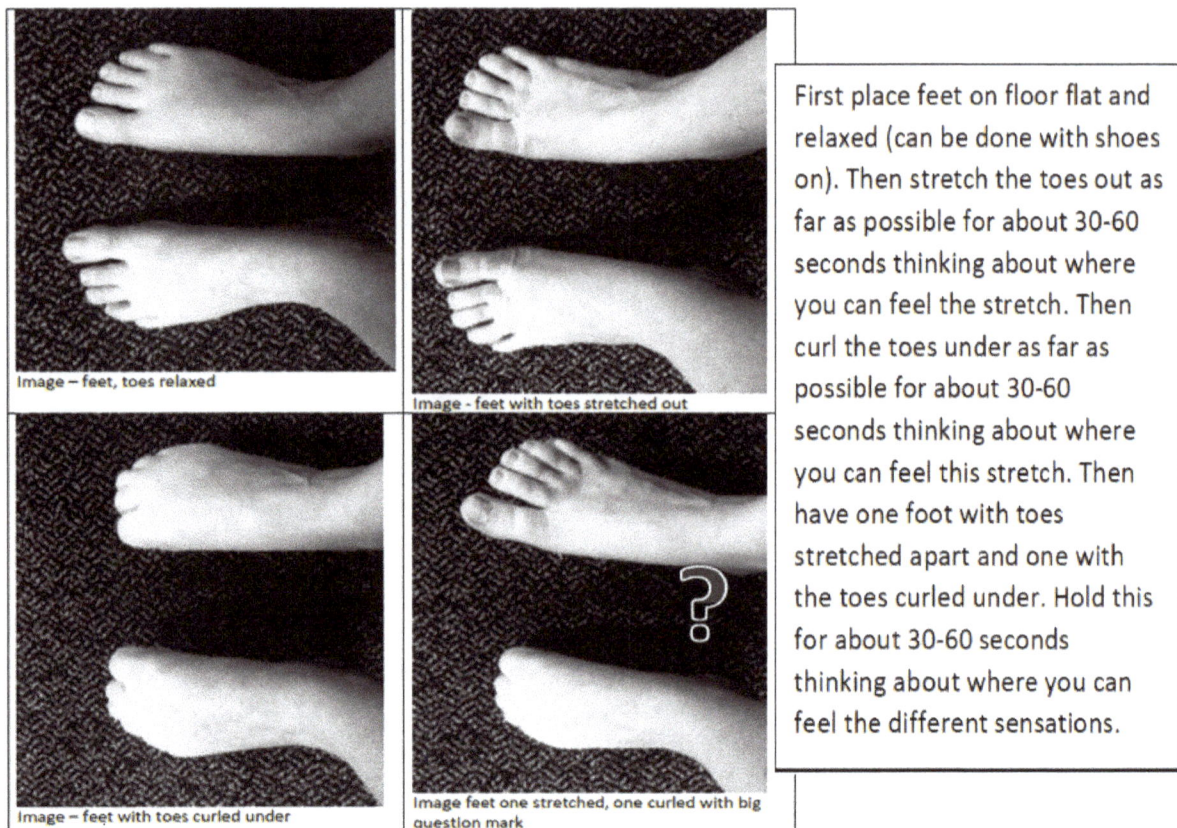

Image – feet, toes relaxed

Image - feet with toes stretched out

Image – feet with toes curled under

Image feet one stretched, one curled with big question mark

First place feet on floor flat and relaxed (can be done with shoes on). Then stretch the toes out as far as possible for about 30-60 seconds thinking about where you can feel the stretch. Then curl the toes under as far as possible for about 30-60 seconds thinking about where you can feel this stretch. Then have one foot with toes stretched apart and one with the toes curled under. Hold this for about 30-60 seconds thinking about where you can feel the different sensations.

Feet stretch and curl - interoception activity
Emma Goodall - Interoception 101 - 2016

The strategy used to prevent an SNS overload occurring MUST be one that the student themselves finds self-calming. Interoception activities will usually work as the focus on the body part is non-threatening and in two years of trials has consistently been shown to lower heart rate, a sign that the parasympathetic nervous system has been activated. This strategy should be implemented as soon as the autistic spectrum students themselves or an adult becomes aware that the child is going into overload. Most autistic spectrum students will have some kind of change that signals they are about to overload, even if they can't identify it themselves yet.

For example, a young girl I worked with would start to vocalise loudly, whereas normally she would vocalise very quietly. Another girl I worked with would become physically tense and give off a distressed vibe. A boy I know will repeat the same phrase over and over (it is a particular phrase) whenever he is becoming anxious to the point of overload. Another boy will start to make big arm movements, whilst another will change his rolling around to jumping from high to low. All these changes are quite subtle but over time, once they know a student well, most teachers can pick up on when an autistic spectrum student is about to meltdown. If you are not yet able to pick up the signs, you can get the whole class to do some interoception activities when key students are off task.

Once the overload has run its course, the autistic spectrum student needs to recover fully before being expected to participate in class. Self-calming strategies such as interoception activities, or access to preferred activities are useful at this point too. Having a safe space to go to, to calm down completely is another option.

Tantrums in autistic spectrum students can be quite spectacular, and do not diminish as quickly as their peers as the students age. The frustration level of autistic spectrum students appears to be higher than their peers for the same frustrations. Thus, a student who does not get a turn on the computer may sulk or protest for five minutes, but an autistic spectrum student may throw a full on thirty-minute tantrum when they do not get a turn on the computer! This may be partly fuelled by the now is forever thinking style of autistics and partly by a lack of interception, meaning that the student does not realise they are frustrated until they are extremely frustrated, and it is too late to calm down easily.

To prevent this kind of distress and promote positive behaviour, it is important for adults to never over promise anything to an autistic spectrum child. Saying, "some of you will get a turn on the computer today, and some of you won't," will be more effective than saying "you should all get a turn on the computer today."

Being seen to be fair will also avoid a lot of potential tantrums, as autistic spectrum students usually become quite distressed or agitated when they perceive an adult as doing something unfair. This can be hard for teachers to understand as some of the autistic spectrum student's own behaviours can be interpreted as unfair, for example, refusing to share colouring pencils with peers or insisting on being at the back of the line all the time.

It is important to ascertain why an autistic spectrum student is doing things that can be seen as unfair, because they will often indicate sensory sensitivities or perfectionism. For example, many autistic spectrum students do not like to share colouring pencils with peers because the other students either break them or don't put them in the container 'the right way'. Being at the back of the line can be a way of preventing unwanted bumps that will occur due to poor awareness of their own body in space.

It used to be said that autistic spectrum children never respond to bribes. This is patently untrue, as any autistic spectrum adult will tell you. However, the type of reward system/bribe that the autistic spectrum student will respond to may be quite specific, individual and unusual. In general, there are two types of rewards and one type of negative consequence that work well for supporting positive behaviour in autistic spectrum students.

The simplest type of reward is socio-emotional, which seems counter intuitive, but it works for me and all of the autistic spectrum adults and children that I know! This is where, when the autistic spectrum child does something you want them to you immediately praise them with very specific language. This praise must say exactly what the child did that you liked and that you either liked it or it made you happy or proud of them. For example:

- "Jonah, I like the way you are sitting quietly. It makes me really happy when you sit quietly."
- "Leila, I like your story writing. I am very proud of you for writing three sentences today."
- "Tom, I like you holding the door for everyone to go through. I like it when I know you are holding the door open nicely."

The other type of reward is the individual and highly specific reward. I have found that the best rewards, which when promised resulted in the biggest improvements in behaviour and compliance are the ones chosen by the autistic spectrum students themselves. One girl, who had not participated in one class discussion for nearly a year, chose a $2 notebook as a reward if she participated in discussions by putting her hand up at least once in each discussion (and responding if she was asked to). This small bribe/reward resulted in the girl becoming an active participant in class discussions more than 75% of the time!

Another autistic spectrum child who was struggling to learn strategies, other than hurting peers who annoyed him, chose 30 minutes iPad time on a particular game. He was given a card to remind him of his new strategy (Stay calm, read a book) and the teacher and teacher aide asked to remind him how he was going to stay calm, whenever they noticed him becoming agitated with peers. Within a few weeks this child was no longer hurting peers and got his 30 minutes iPad time.

I have an aversion to fried food, but when an autistic spectrum student stopped truanting for the last three weeks of a term (after regular truanting all term); I bought him the requested fried food item. He asked for a different reward for the next term, and this too was earned.

Rewards do not need to be given all the time; they can be earned over a period of time. However, the time period needs to work for the child and this should take into account age, emotional maturity and their skills and supports for using the new replacement behaviour. Undesirable behaviours must be replaced and if the autistic spectrum child is not supported to develop desired replacement behaviours then they may well replace it with an even worse behaviour.

Positive Partnerships, an Australian federal initiative, has a useful tool for trying to understand why a particular behaviour might be occurring; the least likely/most likely template. This has been adapted to include the regulation zones from the hand model of the brain and the ANS. The idea is to work out what needs to be in place to guarantee the behaviour will (most likely) or won't happen (least likely):

	People	Place	Activity	Time	Regulation Zone
Most likely	*Who is usually around when the behaviour occurs?*	*Does the behaviour only occur in one (or only a few) places?*	*Think about activities that are happening during; but also, activities immediately prior to, or when the child knows an activity is about to commence*	*Is there a time of day, day of week, etc when the behaviour is likely to occur?*	*Refer to the regulation scale hyperlinked <here>* PANIC ZONE
Least likely	*Who is never around when the behaviour occurs?*	*In what places does the behaviour never occur?*	*What activities are least likely to prompt challenging behaviour?*	*Is there a time when the behaviour is not likely to occur?*	Learning Zone Comfort Zone

Summary of main points – behaviour

1. Ensure environment suits the individual autistic spectrum student's sensory profile where possible
2. Find out what the autistic spectrum student's self-calming strategies are
3. Together identify a safe space for the autistic spectrum student to withdraw to when they need to, and how the student will signal this to you
4. To change behaviours, identify exactly what you want to replace and what with. Communicate this succinctly and precisely to the autistic spectrum student. Provide supports verbally and visually to remind them to use the new behaviour until it becomes a habitual response.
5. Use praise specifically and not generally
6. Rewards need to be seen as motivating by the autistic spectrum student, it is most effective to let them choose their own reward

20

~~~

Resource Links

https://www.youtube.com/channel/UCyIovxevV3W2l2WXHDBkKxA - Healthy Possibilities YouTube channel with interoception and supporting behaviour positively resources.

https://healthypossibilities.net/ is a neurodiversity positive blog written from lived experience. The resources page has a number of useful PowerPoints and videos.

https://mindfulbodyawareness.com/ has a range of resources and products for sale to support the understanding of and development of interoception. Suitable for educators and families.

http://www.setbc.org Special Education Technology – British Columbia website with visual timetables, planners and routines.

http://www.pecs.com/ worldwide site with location specific resources and information.

https://www.youtube.com/user/SingingHandsUK/videos - sign along videos and Makaton resources

http://www.makaton.org.nz/ has information about Makaton in New Zealand and links to resources.

http://www.deaf.co.nz has links to resources for learning sign, including free posters for fingerspelling and numbers.

References

Attwood, T. (2011). The cognitive profile of children who have Asperger's syndrome and the effects on the profile on daily living and the educational curriculum. *Asia Pacific Autism Conference (APAC), Perth, 2011.*

Brugha, T. S., McManus, S., Bankart, J., Scott, F., Purdon, S., Smith, J., ... Meltzer, H. (2011). Epidemiology of autism spectrum disorders in adults in the community in England. *Archive General Psychiatry, 14*(4), 89th ser., 459-465. doi: 10.1001/archgenpsychiatry.2011.38

Bevan-Brown, J., Bourke, R., Butler, P., Carroll-Lind, J., Kearney, A., & Mentis, M. (2011, March). Evaluation of the 'tips for autism' Professional Learning and Development Programme. *Education Counts - An Evaluation of 'tips for Autism'.* Retrieved July 31, 2013, from http://www.educationcounts.govt.nz/__data/assets/pdf_file/0006/105855/Full-Report-Evaluation-of-the-Tips-for-Autism.pdf

Birthday social story [PDF]. (2006). Slater Software Inc.

Brugha, T. S., McManus, S., Bankart, J., Scott, F., Purdon, S., Smith, J., ... Meltzer, H. (2011). Epidemiology of autism spectrum disorders in adults in the community in England. *Archive General Psychiatry, 14*(4), 89th ser., 459-465. doi: 10.1001/archgenpsychiatry.2011.38

Coucouvanis, J. (2005). *Super skills: A social skills group program for children with Asperger syndrome, high-functioning autism and related challenges.* Shawnee Mission, Kan.: Autism Asperger Pub.

Goodall, E. L. (2013). *Five teachers talk about contextual factors involved in teaching students on the autistic spectrum (AS) – a case study* (Doctoral thesis). University Canterbury. Retrieved from http://www.academia.edu/4043471/Five_teachers_talk_about_contextual_factors_involved_in_teaching_students_on_the_autistic_spectrum_AS_-_a_case_study

Lawson, W. (2013). Sensory connection, interest/attention and gamma synchrony in autism or autism, brain connections and preoccupation. *Medical hypotheses, 80*(3), 284-288.

Winter, P. (2013, June 21). What is autism and why do we differ so much? [Web log post]. Retrieved June 21, 2013, from http://strangeringodzone.blogspot.co.nz/2013/06/what-is-autism-and-why-do-we-differ-so.html

Dr Emma Goodall
Emma Goodall 2020

Dr Emma Goodall is an autistic author, keynote speaker, researcher and disability and education consultant. She works both publicly and privately to facilitate the best life outcomes possible for people, including autistics with a range of support needs. She has written and presented on autism, resilience, mental health, interoception, relationships and sexuality for autistics.

An adjunct Professor at the University of Wollongong and on the executive of the Australian Society for Autism Research (ASfAR) Executive Committee, she has developed an online course on managing behaviour positively using interoception for Torrens University and recently collaborated with the Australian Psychological Society to develop an autism specific course for psychologists. Widely published, Emma writes for both academic journals and for mainstream publishers in the areas of autism, disability, education and disability. She has also supported organisations to develop and implement plans to support adult autistics in residential settings.